BECAUSE IT'S THERE
THE LIFE OF GEORGE MALLORY

BECAUSE IT'S THERE
THE LIFE OF GEORGE MALLORY

DUDLEY GREEN

TEMPUS

For my sister Rosemary, my brother Stephen, and in memory of my brother Hugh (1932–1955)

First published 2005

Tempus Publishing Limited
The Mill, Brimscombe Port,
Stroud, Gloucestershire, GL5 2QG
www.tempus-publishing.com

British Library Cataloguing in Publication Data.
A catalogue record for this book is available from the British Library.

ISBN 0 7524 3399 7

Typesetting and origination by Tempus Publishing Limited
Printed in Great Britain

CONTENTS

FOREWORD

BY JOHN MALLORY

I am aware of at least six biographical books about my father, and I found the first edition of Dudley Green's *Mallory of Everest* the one I most enjoyed reading. I have no doubt this new and updated edition will be every bit as good.

When one hears of the many people who now succeed in climbing Mount Everest, one may be tempted to think that the pre-Second World War climbers did not put up too good a show. However, it is always much easier to follow a well-established route than to establish a new one. Obviously the biggest advantage the modern climber has is far better equipment and clothing, especially much lighter and more reliable oxygen apparatus and, above all, the head lamp, which gives climbers much more time for the final push to the summit and the return to their high camp. Even in 1953, the year of the first ascent, they climbed only during the daylight hours.

I am sometimes asked what I think happened on 8 June 1924. There has been much debate as to whether Mallory and Irvine could have climbed the Second Step, the only severe barrier on the route to the summit on that north-east ridge. No one seems to have thought that if they had found it an unclimbable barrier, they would surely have had enough time to return safely to their camp in daylight, so my guess is that they did find a way up, and pushed on, maybe to the summit, far later than would have allowed enough time for a safe descent before dark.

They would almost certainly have used the last of their supplementary oxygen, and would also have been close to the last stages of exhaustion, facing a long and steep descent in fading light. In more recent years a considerable number of climbers have suffered a similar fate, having reached the summit late in the day. Some of their corpses may still be seen on the steep slopes of the mountain.

I stand in awe of what my father and his generation of pioneering Himalayan mountaineers achieved. Whether he and Sandy Irvine reached the summit or not seems to me not supremely important. I tend to share Ed Hillary's view that a successful ascent is not complete without a safe descent.

My great sadness is that I really never knew my father. Yes, I know much about him, but that is not the same.

I hope future generations of mountaineers will learn the importance of being sure to keep an ample reserve of time and energy for a safe descent from whatever mountain they may be climbing.

PREFACE

Mallory: the mere mention of the name is enough to strike a haunting chord in the minds of most adventurous Englishmen and women. For Mallory is part of our national heritage, last seen with Irvine at 28,000ft on Everest 'going strong for the top'. The mystery of his death and the romantic possibility of his ultimate triumph have excited the imagination for eighty years. Ever since as a boy I first heard of that last tantalising glimpse of the two climbers, I have been fascinated by Mallory's story. Later, as I studied his life, I came to realise that there was much more of interest than just the last Everest years. In 1986, the centenary of his birth, I wrote an appreciation of him, which was broadcast on BBC Radio 2, and in 1990 I expanded this into a short account of his life under the title *Mallory of Everest*. I am now grateful to have been given the chance to write a longer biography, which takes into account the discovery of Mallory's body and the results of subsequent investigations on the mountain.

No one can study the life of George Mallory without being heavily indebted to the works of previous writers, and especially the biography written in 1969 by his son-in-law, David Robertson, a scholarly work which quotes extensively from his letters, writings and other family records. I have also made use of the earlier memoir by David Pye, which appeared in 1927. The detailed account of the early Everest expeditions by Tom Holzel and Audrey Salkeld (second edition, 1999) has been of great value to me and I have also consulted Peter and Leni Gillman's study of Mallory's life published in 2000. The discovery of Mallory's body in 1999 by the Mallory and Irvine Research Expedition has been fully documented in two outstanding books. *Ghost of Everest* is an account of the 1999 expedition, while *Detectives on Everest* records the expedition's further researches on the mountain in 2001 and provides a detailed analysis of the implications.

I should like to express my thanks to all who have assisted me in my research for this volume. I owe a great debt of gratitude to Audrey Salkeld, who invited me to stay at her Lake District home and shared with me her vast knowledge of the Everest story. Audrey and her husband Peter also gave me invaluable assistance over the provision of photographs. I am grateful to Dick Norton for his kind hospitality and for allowing me to see his father's fine watercolours of Everest and his climbing diary. I should like to thank Sandra Noel who invited me to her home in Kent to see her father's wonderful photographic collection. I am grateful to George Mallory's grandson, George Millikan, for making available two photographs of his grandfather. I should also like to thank Robin Ashcroft, manager of the National Mountaineering Exhibition at Rheged, Penrith, for his hospitality.

I should like to repeat the thanks which I expressed in 1990 to members of the Mallory family who allowed me to make use of their family records: to Clare Millikan, George Mallory's daughter, who kindly supplied me with a photograph of her mother; to Molly Dalglish, daughter of George's sister Avie, for allowing me to borrow family photographs; to her brother, Ben Longridge, and his wife Stella, for permitting me to make use of their family records; to Barbara Newton Dunne, daughter of George's elder sister Mary, who put at my disposal the letters George wrote home from school, and allowed me to select from her collection of family photographs.

I should also like to express my thanks once again to Kate Willert and Jane O'Malley, daughters of George's climbing friend Cottie Sanders, who in 1990 gave me constant support and encouragement. Mrs Willert welcomed me into her London home and allowed me to study her mother's Mallory letters and her climbing diaries; Miss O'Malley answered many of my queries and provided much much valuable information. I am grateful to Mr Michael Sissons and Miss Margaret Stephens for enabling me to establish this contact.

For the earlier period of Mallory's life I should like to repeat my thanks to those who assisted me in my initial research: Mr J.T. Hopkins and Miss J.M. Williams of Cheshire Record Office; the Revd Michael Graham,

Rector of Mobberley; Mr Roger Custance, archivist of Winchester College; Mrs Mary Coleman, assistant librarian of the Pepys Library, Magdalene College, Cambridge; and Mr Tony Palmer of the Cambridge University Board of Extra-mural Studies. I am also grateful to my cousin, Christopher Olpherts, who undertook research on my behalf at Winchester, and to Mrs Ann Williams, Librarian of Charterhouse, for her warm welcome when I visited the school in 1990 and for supplying much information about Mallory's time as a master there.

For the Everest years I have made considerable use of the official expedition accounts. I am very grateful to Rachel Swann of the Alpine Club Picture Library for her warm welcome and assistance over my selection of photographs. I should also like to record my gratitude to the officers of the club who assisted me in my initial researches in 1990: Mr Bob Lawford, honorary librarian, for his guidance over illustrations; Mr Edward Smyth, honorary archivist and long-time friend of my family, for his kind hospitality and for initiating my research at the club and making available Mallory's correspondence with Geoffrey Winthrop Young; and Mrs Pat Johnson, for her assistance in the library.

I should like to thank Justin Hobson and Joy Wheeler of the Royal Geographical Society Picture Library for their advice over pho-tographs. And once again I should like to record my gratitude to Christine Kelly, who, as archivist of the Royal Geographical Society, gave me a warm welcome in 1990 and guided my initial research into the Everest archives. My thanks are due to Mr John Burgess, assistant librarian of Merton College, Oxford, who made available the Irvine material and gave me assistance with photographs. I am also greatly indebted to David Rayvern Allen of the BBC, for his willingness in 1986 to use my original Mallory script.

I should like to repeat my gratitude to the following who in 1990 answered my queries or assisted my initial research: Mrs Eleanor Wynthrop Young, Mr Francis Nevel, Mr Robert Longridge, Mr Bill Summers, Miss Cathy Henderson (research librarian of the Harry Ransom Humanities Research Centre, University of Texas, USA), Dr D.M. Owen and Dr P.N.R. Zutshi of the University Archives, Cambridge, Mrs Ruth Brown of Westbrook, Mr Gavin Stamp, Brigadier Geoffrey Gathercole (formerly deputy director of the Royal

Geographical Society), Mr John Knight of the BBC, Miss Mavis Pindard of Faber and Faber and Mr Kai Ken Yung of the National Portrait Gallery. I am also grateful to my friend Brian Elcox for his meticulous care in reading my text and to Brian Lee for his great skill in reproducing many of the photographs.

I should like to record my gratitude to Dr Ron Freethy, whose vision and enthusiasm made possible the publication of my earlier work, *Mallory of Everest*, and to thank Ron and his wife Marlene for their continued support and advice. I also owe a great debt to my brother Stephen. He has been a fount of information on many points of reference and has always been willing to assist my research. I am grateful to him for his encouragement and support and for reading my manuscript and making numerous helpful suggestions. I should also like to thank James Howarth, Holly Bennion and Rob Sharman of Tempus Publishing for their kind assistance. I am especially grateful to James for his vision in seeing the possibility of publishing a revised and enlarged version of my earlier work on George Mallory.

I should also like to place on record my special thanks to Jochen Hemmleb of the Mallory and Irvine Research Expeditions for reading my manuscript account of the discovery of Mallory's body and for making several suggestions to bring the account up to date and to ensure greater accuracy. He went far beyond the call of duty in his response to my request and I am very grateful to him. Finally, my deepest gratitude goes to John Mallory for writing a foreword to this book and also for providing the photograph of the slate plaque erected in May 1995 in memory of all who died on the early Everest expeditions. It was a privilege to entertain him in May 2004 during his visit to England to mark the eightieth anniversary of his father's disappearance.

The discovery of Mallory's body in 1999 has led to renewed fascination with the story of Everest. I hope that the publication of this biography will play its part in fostering that interest, both in the early British expeditions and also in the character of the man who more than any other has been associated with the mountain.

Dudley Green
Clitheroe, May 2005

PICTURE CREDITS

I am grateful to the following individuals and institutions for permission to reproduce illustrations:

The Alpine Club Photo Library for nos 18, 23, 25, 31, 32, 33, 37, 55 and 56; David Breashears for nos 57 and 58; Dr Ron Freethy for no.54; the Warden and Fellows of Merton College, Oxford, for nos 46 and 51; the Millican family for nos 13 and 30; the Rector of Mobberley for no.4; the John Noel Photographic Collection for nos 38, 48, 49, 50, 52 and 53; the Master and Fellows of Magdalene College, Cambridge for no.15; and the Salkeld Collection for no.47.

ONE

BOYHOOD: MOBBERLEY AND WINCHESTER 1886-1905

The flat Cheshire plain may seem an unlikely setting for the birthplace of a great mountaineer, but it was in the pleasant, straggling village of Mobberley that George Mallory was born on 18 June 1886. His father, the Revd Herbert Leigh Mallory, had been appointed rector of the parish in the previous year, on the death of George's grandfather, who himself had been rector for fifty-three years. The name Mallory came from George's grandmother's side of the family, who had had a long-standing connection with the village. They had been lords of the manor for over 200 years, and for most of that time they had supplied the rectors of the parish. Mobberley church, dedicated to St Wilfrid, is a fine example of late medieval work. It contains a magnificent sixteenth-century rood screen and also many memorials to the Mallory family.

In 1832 George's grandfather, the Revd George Leigh, married Julia, the only child of the Revd John Mallory, the last surviving male member of the Mallory family. His father-in-law died that same year and, on his appointment as rector of Mobberley, George Leigh adopted by royal licence the right to use the surname of Mallory. His son, Herbert Leigh Mallory, succeeded to the rectorship in 1895. The youngest of ten children, he had been educated at King William's College in the Isle of Man and at Trinity College, Cambridge. He had been ordained in 1879 and had served curacies in Cambridge, Market Harborough in Leicestershire and Great Haseley in Oxfordshire.

In 1882 he had married Annie Beridge Jebb, the posthumous daughter of the Revd John Beridge Jebb of Walton Lodge, Chesterfield.

Herbert and Annie had four children: Mary, George, Avie and Trafford. Surrounded by a background of love and affection, the Mallory children enjoyed a happy childhood. They were given considerable freedom by their parents and indulged in many adventurous escapades. Years later George's sister Avie recalled that it was always fun to be with him, for he had the knack of making things exciting:

> He climbed everything that it was at all possible to climb. I learnt very early that it was fatal to tell him that any tree was impossible for him to get up. 'Impossible' was a word which acted as a challenge to him. When he once told me that it would be quite easy to lie between the railway lines and let a train go over him, I kept very quiet, as if I thought it would be a very ordinary thing to do; otherwise I was afraid he would do it. He used to climb up the downspouts of the house, and climb about on the roof with cat-like surefootedness.

Avie also remembered that as children they used to ride wildly round on bicycles from which they had removed all such surplus weight as mudguards, bells and brakes, and that, after one particularly hair-raising episode, George's only comment was that it was no good, they would have to put the bell back on. At the age of seven George was found climbing on the roof of the church, after he had been banished from the nursery for unruly behaviour. There was also a memorable occasion on a family holiday at St Bees, when he was seen perched on a rock, cut off by the incoming tide. He had waited to see whether the tide would cover the top of this rock and he was now in a situation of considerable danger. It was only with some difficulty, and with the help of a bystander, that he was eventually brought to the shore.

On another occasion the children followed a route along the shore under the cliffs. They were expected to arrive back in time for a picnic tea, but it was a long way and as the tide came in they got into difficulties. At one point George had to lower himself into the water between two rocks to enable the others to use his shoulder as a stepping-stone. It was dark before they reached home to find that a search party had already set out to look for them. The children's only regret was that they had missed their tea.

After a short time at school in West Kirby, George was sent to Glengorse, a preparatory school in Eastbourne. He seemed happy there and each week cheerful letters addressed to 'My dear Mater' arrived at the rectory. On 14 February 1897 he reported:

> I had my first experience of football on Friday, it was a very nice experi-
> ence. The first damage I did was to charge two boys over on their faces,
> the second was to kick the ball into a boy's nose and the third damage was
> to charge a boy over on his ribs.

He went on to say that there was only one boy, out of the fifty-four in the school, the son of the school matron, who was 'at all nasty'. He settled in so well that it came as a surprise when he ran away from the school two years later. But it seems that he only did this to help a friend, who did not feel up to running away on his own. The two boys were quickly traced and the master who brought them back was intrigued to notice that George's luggage, wrapped up in a brown paper parcel, contained nothing but his geometry books. He agreed with the boys that if they returned to school they would not be punished. But on their return, much to George's disgust, they were given a sound beating. When George told the story in later life he made it clear that this betrayal of faith still rankled in his mind.

George's early love of geometry soon bore fruit. In the summer of 1900 he won a mathematics scholarship to Winchester College. Within a few days of his arrival at the school he reported to his mother:

> I like being here very much – ever so much better than Glengorse; and I like
> the men better too. (Instead of chaps we always say men.) We have plenty of
> work to do, and I'm afraid I'm running you up a heavy book bill. [...] We
> get up at 6.15 and begin work – morning lines its called – at 7.00.

A few days later he wrote:

It's simply lovely being here; life is like a dream. I enjoy it immensely. [...]
I spend most of our afternoon time reading in our library. [...]

P.S. Please tell Trafford from me that he must buck up and become
a mathematician, and if he can't read decently by next hols I shall kick
him.

George threw himself into the varied life of the school with
great vigour. Although he showed little skill at cricket, he was a
keen member of College VI, playing at full-back in the Winchester
version of inter-house six-a-side football. A friend recalled that he
played with great enthusiasm and did not like to lose. An account of
a match between College VI and House VI in December 1904 reports
that 'Mallory was quite good, busting [kicking] extremely well'. His
best sport was gymnastics. He worked hard on the horizontal bar
and became one of the finest gymnasts in the school. In June 1902
he told his mother:

I do a great deal of gymna and enjoy myself thoroughly. Yesterday I managed
to do for the first time a thing which I have been trying since the end of
last half without success, and which I am particularly pleased at getting
because no one else in the school can do it.

He enjoyed attending the play-readings given by Montague Rendall,
the second master, and also developed an interest in visiting ancient
churches. On one occasion he went with his sister Avie to Winchester
Cathedral. Finding a small door in the tower unlocked, they climbed
the steps and came upon an old man just about to wind up the clock:
to their great delight they were allowed to do it for him. In May 1904
George went on an energetic outing to Salisbury Cathedral, which he
later described to Avie:

I went to Salisbury on Ascension Day and liked it very much outside, but
thought it rather a good thing spoilt inside. Eddy Morgan came with me in
a trailer, as he is not allowed to bike far; and, as the road was up and down
precipices for about 27 miles, I fairly sweated.

Although he worked conscientiously, George was not an outstand-ing scholar. He was entered in the Army Class but it seems that he had no ambition for a military career. Shortly before the 1904 examina-tions for the Royal Military Academy, Woolwich, he confided to his sister Mary that he did not want to pass and in the event he failed by a narrow margin.

In July 1904 George was delighted to take part in a notable school triumph. He was a member of the Winchester shooting VIII which won the Ashburton Shield at Bisley. It was a very close contest: with his final shot the last man gained the bull's-eye which won the event for Winchester. George, who had been the best shot over 2,000 yards, wrote an exultant report to his sister Avie:

> It was simply glorious! We won the Public School Racquets last holidays, we badly beat Eton at cricket, and now we have won the Public Schools Shooting which is really the best of the lot, because every decent school goes in for it, and it comes into public notice much more than anything else. There was a great crowd at Bisley on Thursday, and I think our win was very popular.
>
> When we arrived at the station here about eight o'clock in the evening, we found the whole school waiting to receive us. We were seized and carried to a brake which was waiting to drive us down; and we started a procession, the Militia band in front playing 'See the conquering heroes come' – though I didn't hear a note of it because of the cheering, which continued the whole way down from the station.
>
> As soon as the brake drew up at Commoner Gate by the headmaster's house, we were again seized and carried to Flint Court [the three-sided quadrangle surrounded by classrooms]: then Burge [the headmaster] came and made a very nice speech, there was more prolonged cheering, and the band made another noise. After that, I was carried into College, where I was rescued by Rendell, who came and congratulated me and asked me to go and have some supper with him.

In retrospect, however, the most important effect that Winchester had on George was that there he came into contact with Graham Irving, a young master who had recently come down from New

College, Oxford. Irving was an enthusiastic and highly accomplished mountaineer, who was a keen exponent of climbing in the Alps without using the services of a guide, a custom at that time deplored by many older mountaineers. In 1904 the friend with whom he had done most of his climbing had recently died, and he decided to recruit some Winchester lads and train them as climbing companions. As he later told the Alpine Club:

> It wasn't hard to do so; living in rooms almost adjoining mine were the very persons I wanted. The enlistment of my first recruit took place on the occasion of my finding him developing photographs during illicit hours. A tactful remark of his about a Swiss photograph led to an amicable discussion.

This first recruit was Harry Gibson, who had been to Zermatt and Grindelwald with his father. Harry then enlisted the support of George Mallory. The two were firm friends and the finest gymnasts in the school. Graham Irving invited both boys to accompany him on an Alpine holiday that summer. George, aware that his parents might be worried over the expense of this venture, wrote diplomatically to his mother to get her agreement:

> I am quite aware that cash is very scarce just now, which makes my expedition to Switzerland seem rather a nuisance. The only expense will be the ticket out there; I don't know how much that will come to, but I hope Gra[n] will give me something towards that – by way of a birthday present – ; then too the cost of keeping me at home for the three weeks or whatever it is that I am in Switzerland would amount to something considerable, so that if you reckon the cost of the expedition from that point of view it will come to something very small I fancy.

After securing the consent of their families both lads threw themselves enthusiastically into their preparations, practising climbing in the ruins of Wolvesey Castle, the original palace of the bishops of Winchester.

They left for Switzerland at the beginning of August. After arriving in Martigny on the 4th, they went on to Bourg St Pierre, intending to climb Mont Vélan the next day. George's Alpine career, however, had a rather inglorious start, for on the ascent of this first peak both boys suffered badly from mountain sickness and had to abandon the climb just 600ft below the summit. But, nothing daunted, they continued with their programme and three days later they reached the summit of the Grand Combin. George wrote in triumph to his mother:

> Yesterday morning we started at six o'clock and went straight up over snow slopes and shaly rock to about 11,700ft – a very tiring proceeding. About 500ft of rather good rock climbing then brought us to the west arête of the mountain. From here we had a most interesting and in parts fairly difficult rock climb up the west arête, which we followed for about 1800ft... After this we traversed to the right, had a little more rock climbing and then cut up a steep ice slope, which brought us nearly to the top of the Valsorey Combin. After this we were on snow the whole time. We descended 400ft of snow slope and had a rest and a grub, and then went up the last 700ft in fine form in half an hour. The Grand Combin is 14,100 feet, and of course the view from the top is perfectly ripping.

In high spirits they descended to Mauvoisin in the Val de Bagnes. Irving later recalled their feelings:

> I am sure three happier men never went to bed in Switzerland. The Vélan was forgotten; its gloom had been swallowed up in the sunshine of the Combin. In dealing with rock, snow and even ice, my recruits had performed wonders; they had won their spurs, and the great world above the snow-line was ours to conquer and enjoy.

On 10 August they took the High Level Route to Staffelalp and arrived in Zermatt after a seventeen-hour day. Three days later they climbed the Dufourspitze (15,217ft), the highest peak of Monte Rosa, and descended to Gressoney in Italy. Gibson, whose turn it was to keep the party's journal, noted their reception:

> Refused admittance as disreputable at the best hotel, we got a much needed supper and promise of 'a sofa and two beds' in the parlour of another. the sofa was a fairly normal bed; the two beds were a single straw-stuffed

mattress shaped something like the Matterhorn, from which the pillow slid owing to the angle. Nevertheless, we all slept the sleep of the just.

They recrossed the border by the Felikjoch pass and returned to Zermatt. Harry Gibson then had to return home.

On 18 August, in very bad weather, Irving and Mallory crossed into France by the Col de Balme and went on to Chamonix. Their intention was to climb Mont Blanc, but for the next week they were frustrated by heavy snowfalls and exceptionally high winds. At last on 26 August the wind seemed to have dropped and they set out from the Dôme hut at 7 a.m. They ascended the west branch of the Dôme glacier and started up the ridge which connects the Aiguilles Grises with the Bionnassay arête. Irving recorded their ascent:

> The wind had swept all the snow off, and the leader found his crampons of great assistance. GHLM managed with great skill to get up with a minimum of steps, and excellent progress was made along the narrow Bionassay arête till we reached the flank of the Dôme. Here we met the wind, which made us feel as if we had absolutely nothing on. Mallory suffered severely, and his legs seemed likely to freeze altogether. We took shelter for a bit under the wall of a crevasse and, when the gale abated, made our way across to the Vallot hut, which was reached soon after twelve o'clock.

After a meal of soup and bread they started up the Bosses du Dromadaire. Irving commented:

> Down at Chamonix, far below, we could fancy the telescope men getting their placards to hang round their instruments: 'Des messieurs sont visibles au Mont Blanc.' What none of those men down below could feel was the thrill in the hearts of those two small specks slowly crawling up the steep ice, and at times pressed close against it to prevent being blown off by the freezing gale that still blew.

They reached the summit after an hour and a quarter. On the descent, George, who had no crampons and was almost numb with cold, slipped and dragged Irving from his footing, but after a short slide they checked their fall and continued none the worse. They reached Chamonix just before 9 p.m. and consumed an enormous meal at Couttet's Hotel. A few days later George returned home to rejoin his family. He had had a wide range of mountaineering experiences and his Alpine education had truly begun.

That winter Graham Irving founded the Ice Club at Winchester. He himself was the first president and the other members were Harry Gibson, George Mallory, Guy Bullock and Harry Tyndale. They showed great enthusiasm, calling each other by the names of famous Alpine guides. Years later Harry Tyndale recalled catching Mallory's eye in chapel whenever they reached the appropriate passages in the *Benedicite*: 'O ye ice and snow... O ye mountains and hills, bless ye the Lord.'

Although at home the mountains were not immediately accessible, George continued to practise climbing whenever possible. His family had now moved to Birkenhead, where his father had been appointed vicar of St John's Church. Harold Porter, a friend who stayed with George at Birkenhead, later described his climbing activities on the vicarage roof:

> His idea was to get out of the bedroom window, whence he could balance up to grasp the overhanging eaves and with an acrobatic kick and swing attain the roof. I was to hold him on a rope from inside the bedroom. All went according to plan, except that his acrobatic kick somehow touched the window pane, which crashed with a loud noise. His mother, who was a bit of an invalid and was having a siesta next door, quite unaware of our activities, rushed in to find me paying out the rope as George sped over the roof to a known route of descent on the far side, leaving to me the embarrassing task of pacifying his agitated parent until his reappearance.

On an excursion from Winchester, George also climbed the tower of the old abbey church at Romsey.

Throughout his last year at Winchester, George was working hard to win a scholarship at Cambridge and he was delighted to gain an exhibition in history at Magdalene College. He celebrated the last day of the summer term by climbing up between the tower of the gate into Chamber Court and a chimney. There was a sheer drop below and one school fellow later recalled that the sight of it made him feel almost sick, while another said that it looked like magic.

At the beginning of August, the Ice Club set out for Switzerland for a second Alpine season. Although their activities were slightly restricted by the presence of ladies in the party and by some indifferent weather, they spent an enjoyable month climbing from Arolla. Their most notable achievement was a speedy ascent of the Dent Blanche. George wrote to his mother describing the climb:

> At 3.15 yesterday morning we started by moonlight across the huge snow field, on the most delightful hard crisp snow; and after the most enjoyable walk and a short scramble over easy rocks, we found ourselves on the arête of the Dent Blanche at 7.15. The sun of course had risen as we neared the Dent Blanche; and, as we had already gone up quite a lot, the view was splendid right over the Mont Blanc range. It was altogether too inexpressibly glorious to see peak after peak touched with the pink glow of the first sun which slowly spread until the whole top was a flaming fire – and that against a sky with varied tints of leaden blue.
>
> We had a halt and breakfast for nearly an hour on the arête and then climbed straight to the top in a little over three hours, arriving there at 10.25. [...] We had no difficulty coming down, but a most laborious walk across the snow field. The rest of the party were waiting tea for us at the Bertol hut as prearranged, and rejoiced with our rejoicing – the Dent Blanche was the one peak we had set our hearts upon doing.

At the end of the month George returned to England to prepare for his new life at Cambridge.

TWO

CAMBRIDGE 1905-1909

On the Sunday before the start of Michaelmas Term 1905, Mr Arthur Benson, who had recently been appointed supervisor in history at Magdalene College, Cambridge, attended Matins in King's College Chapel. There were not many in the congregation and his attention was struck by a youthful-looking undergraduate in a new gown who was sitting just in front of him. He was following the order of service very reverently, standing or kneeling in the appropriate places while most of the congregation remained seated throughout. Soon after returning to his rooms in the Old Granary, a short distance from the college, a Mr Mallory, one of his pupils in history, was announced. In their discussion about his studies for the coming term, George showed great enthusiasm for his subject and said he was keen to develop his essay-writing skills. Benson noted in his diary:

> I had noticed in King's in the morning a fine looking boy, evidently a fresh-man, just in front of me – lo and behold the same came to call on me, and turns out to be Mallory, from Winchester, one of our new exhibitioners at Magdalene. He sat sometime; and a simpler, more ingenuous, more unaffected, more genuinely interested boy, I never saw.

Arthur Christopher Benson was the eldest son of Edward White Benson, Archbishop of Canterbury from 1883 to 1896. He had been educated at Eton and King's College, Cambridge, and, after a short spell as a master at Eton, had been elected a Fellow at Magdalene in 1903. He had a reputation as a poet and essayist and in 1902 had written the Coronation Ode, which included the famous 'Land of Hope and Glory', for which Elgar composed the music. He was also the author of a two-volume biography of his father and in 1914 he was to become the Master of Magdalene College.

Benson took a keen personal interest in George's progress and encouraged him to read as widely as possible, advising him that: 'In reading the best rule is to read what interests one, as long, of course, as the books are good and not merely trivial.' George devoted a lot of time to his essays and often wrote at such length that he could not finish in time. On one occasion a massive essay arrived so late that Benson had no chance of reading it before George himself arrived. Benson spoke sharply to him, saying that such persistent lateness destroyed his pleasure in reading the essay and his ability to discuss it. George contritely expressed his apologies and Benson later discovered that he had become so interested in the topic that he had sat up all night writing the essay.

At that time Magdalene College consisted of about fifty under-graduates and formed a small and friendly community. George threw himself wholeheartedly into college life. He assisted Benson with the founding of the Kingsley Club, a college society for the reading of papers and the holding of informal debates. Although not a deep thinker, he was an enthusiastic and somewhat impatient debater. He spoke very rapidly and had the rather annoying tendency of insisting, however flimsy his grounds, that any honest and clear-headed man must agree with him. His friend David Pye later recalled:

> In spite of his impatience in argument it was impossible to be either bored or angry, for his irritability was never prolonged beyond the limits of debate. The wrangle finished, he was all friendly interest and consideration. I think he regarded debatable questions as providing a sort of intellectual fisticuffs in which you hit out as shrewdly as you could and did not resent your adversary doing the same. In all ordinary matters he was delightfully good-humoured and tolerant.

During his second year George made many contacts outside his own college. In February 1907 he dined at Christ's College where he met Charles Sayle, the under-librarian at the university library. Sayle, who was also a founder member of the Climbers' Club, took delight in fostering the intellectual social life at Cambridge, and regularly held court at his rooms at 8 Trumpington Street. He described the young men who congregated there as 'his swans' and he invited George to become a regular member of the group.

George now found himself drawn into a close-knit circle of friends, who took a keen interest in politics and shared a love of literature and the arts. They included Geoffrey Keynes of Pembroke College, later to achieve distinction as a scientist and surgeon, and his brother, Maynard, the eminent economist; Hugh Wilson and the poet, Rupert Brooke, of King's; and James Strachey and David Pye of Trinity. Under their influence George joined the recently founded Cambridge University Fabian Society, and also served as college secretary on the committee of the university Women's Suffrage Association.

In November 1907, when the newly formed Marlowe Society gave a production of *Doctor Faustus*, George gave an enthusiastic rendering of the Pope, while Rupert Brooke played Mephistopheles and Geoffrey Keynes the Evil Angel. It was about this time, according to David Pye, that he took to dressing rather peculiarly in black flannel shirts and coloured ties, and grew his hair long. Cottie Sanders, who later became a climbing friend of George, met several of the group and considered that they formed what she termed the Cambridge School of Friendship. She considered that their influence left its mark on George in the serious and conscientious way in which he treated friendship:

They held personal relationships as so important that they held only a few other things as being of any importance whatsoever. Conventional inessentials simply had no meaning for them. They were extraordinarily attached to one another; they stuck closer than brothers; there was, literally, nothing that they wouldn't do for one another. They enjoyed each other furiously; delightedly, they examined and explored every means of knowing people better and liking them more, from the simplest pleasures of food and exercise taken together to the final closeness of the common acceptance of some sorrow or some truth.

George's main recreation at Cambridge was rowing. He represented the college in each of his first three years, and was elected captain of the college boat club for 1907/08. That year was the most successful in the history of Magdalene rowing. The college gained four places in the Lent races and five in the Mays. This success prompted them to contemplate sending an eight to the Henley Regatta, and George circulated a letter asking for financial contributions to make this possible. An eight was sent to Henley which put up a good performance both in the Ladies' Plate and the Thames Challenge Cup.

Although Cambridge had nothing to offer in the way of mountains, George enjoyed the wide open spaces of the fens. He made several excursions in the company of David Pye, who later recalled some of their expeditions:

> One long day we spent on the river at St. Ives. We rowed up a much reed-grown channel to Houghton, and watched a huge dripping mill-wheel, with the sweet scent of the fresh river water all about it. Then we took the other arm of the river, and by dint of carrying the boat round a deserted lock, got to Hemingford Grey and Hemingford Abbots, two quiet villages with fine churches close to the river, and a view over the wide alluvial plain of the Ouse. Other days were spent more energetically afoot, tracing the prehistoric earthworks with which the uplands towards Newmarket abound, or following the whole course of the Via Devana where it flings away, a green and crinkly riband over the Gog Magog hills, straight to some forgotten goal.

George was determined to continue his climbing activities and in September 1907, at the end of his second year at Cambridge, he arranged a holiday in Snowdonia with Geoffrey Keynes and Hugh Wilson. They stayed at Gwern-y-Gof Uchaf, a farm near Capel Curig, and for a week they climbed every day on Tryfan, Y Lliwedd, Craig yr Isfa and Glyder Fawr. Unwittingly they made one entry into the record books. While climbing the Central Route of Lliwedd's East

Buttress one of the party dislodged a large rock which crashed down the cliff, narrowly missing Archer Thomson, one of the most distinguished figures in Welsh climbing, who was making the first ascent of a new route. He delivered a stern rebuke to the party and then decided to call his new climb 'Avalanche Route'. Writing to a friend, Hugh Wilson described their activities in glowing terms:

> We didn't see the sunrise, I fear. But for seven mornings did we bathe in a mountain stream by the farm house at about 7.15am, start for our mountain 8.30, bathe in some lake before our climb, climb until four or five in the afternoon, bathe on our way back – oh such bathes; and get home absolutely worn out with air and exercise in time for supper at 7.30. Tea at 8.30, bed before 9.00. Isn't it a good life?

Looking back later, Geoffrey Keynes thought that the ten days they had spent in Wales had been the best of his life and Hugh Wilson wondered whether such a time could ever occur again. In August the following year, George cycled to North Wales with his brother Trafford for another climbing holiday at Capel Curig, and then in September he spent nine days at in the Lake District staying at Wasdale Head with Geoffrey Keynes, Harry Gibson and Harold Porter. They climbed most of the well-known routes in the district and added new climbs on the Ennerdale face of Great Gable.

George's passion for bathing, regardless of the circumstances or the temperature of the water, nearly landed him in trouble at Cambridge. While out punting with some friends on one hot night during the long vacation, he insisted on diving into the water some way below Magdalene Bridge, despite the protests of his companions that they had to return the punt by ten o'clock. When he refused to get back into the boat his friends made off up the river. Thinking that he could get into college via the Fellows' Garden, George made no attempt to follow them, but he found all the doors to be locked and was unable to attract anyone's attention. Finally, in desperation, he swam across to the quayside and sprinted naked over the bridge to the college gates. He knocked furiously at the door but before the porter could open up a policeman appeared and demanded his name. After some discussion the policeman agreed that no further action would be taken provided that George was reported to the college authorities.

At the end of May 1907 George sat the first of his Cambridge examinations, part one of the history tripos. He felt quite confident of the result, telling Benson: 'I am always happiest on the eve of the fray – it is a stimulus which suits me.' But his confidence was misplaced for, when the results were published three weeks later, he found that, although he had been awarded high marks for his essay, he had been placed in the third class. Although at this time the majority of Cambridge undergraduates only sat for a pass degree George dismissed this as 'a worthless performance'. Arthur Benson blamed himself, saying that he had allowed him to read too widely and spend too much time on his essays. He invited George to stay the last week of June with him at Hinton Hall, a large house which he had rented in the fens at Haddenham, near Ely. Each day they made excursions into the countryside. Benson had recently bought a car and his chauffeur took them for drives across the fens. On other occasions they went out for cycle rides. George wrote home expressing his enjoyment:

> It is a jolly place to stay. One generally arrives back in time for a late tea, after which ACB produces gems of literature and we both read until dinner at 8.15. After dinner he plays a delightful little organ which he possesses and I (not at the same time) a pianola. But the joy of the place is that one can do exactly as one likes, and everything is so peaceful and quiet and comfortable.

George continued to work hard at his studies and he was pleased that in part two of the history tripos he was placed in the second class. On the basis of this result he decided to return to Cambridge for a fourth year. He took rooms in Pythagoras House, an old building near the northern end of the Backs and not far from Magdalene College. He devoted much of his time to the preparation of an essay on Dr Johnson's biographer, James Boswell, which he submitted for the Members' Prize Essay. His essay received favourable comment and, although he did not win the prize, he was encouraged to expand it for publication as a book.

Mr Mellory

Easter Term 190*8*

Magdalene College, Cambridge.

With Mr A. G. Peskett's Compliments.

☞ This Bill must be paid *on or before* coming into residence next Term.

No Student whose account is in arrear can be permitted to continue in residence, nor can any College Certificate for Degree or other purpose be granted him.

Mr Peskett's Bankers are Barclay and Company, Limited, Mortlock's Bank, Cambridge, whose Head Office is at 54, Lombard Street, E.C. When money is paid to Mr Peskett's Bankers, it is particularly requested that the name of the Pupil on whose account it is paid may be accurately stated; and also *that no payment be made in any other way than through the Bankers.*

Payments can also be made through any of the Branches of Barclay and Company, Limited.

The accounts at this College are kept by *Terms* and not by *Quarters,* consequently all the regular yearly payments are divided into *three* instead of *four* equal parts.

Residence for next Term will begin on the 12 *October* and every Undergraduate is strictly required to be in College by that day.

To Credit.	£	s.	d.
Balance from last Account			
Scholarship or Exhibition			
Benefaction *Balance of Grant for Architect Fee*	3	0	0
Valuation			
Remission from Tuition	2	0	0
	5	0	0

Cambridge, *Nov 9/08*
We have placed £ *37-12-10*
to the Account of Mr Peskett for
Barclay and Company, Limited.

	£	s.	d.
Bedmaker	2	2	0
College Servant	1	5	0
Laundress	1	12	6
Matriculation Fee			
Examination Fee			
Degree Fees	5	1	0
Coals		7	6
Rent			
Steward's Account	2	19	11
Establishment	5	0	0
Tutorial Fund	3	10	0
Private Tutor			
Public Lectures	2	2	0
Lodgings			
Cash			
College Amalgamation Club	1	10	0
Hall Dinners	6	6	8
Cook	10	9	3
Painter and Glazier			
Carpenter			
Smith			
Surgeon		7	0
Upholsterer			
Valuation of Rooms			
Total of Term	42	12	10
Credit	5	0	0
Balance due	37	12	10

Turn over

George's college bill for Easter 1908.

During this final year George showed great kindness and understanding towards Arthur Benson, who after prolonged attacks of melancholy had been obliged to leave Cambridge for a lengthy period of rest. He had returned in October 1908 but was still constantly prone to fits of depression and, although he managed to get through his college duties, he shunned the society of his friends. During this time he was greatly struck by the support and encouragement which he received from Mallory. As David Pye later wrote:

> He was the only undergraduate of that time, so Mr Benson told me, who constantly and continually, week after week, put himself out to do what he could to help. He used to come in to see him, and to arrange to go out walking or bicycling, at least twice a week. He would talk about the sort of matters he thought would be of interest and would invite him to his rooms to meet men in whom he would be interested.

It says much for George's sympathy and patience that he was willing to spend so much time in the company of a man old enough to be his father, who was plunged into deep melancholy for much of the time and was often hardly able to sustain any conversation at all. David Pye was told by Arthur Benson how Mallory would entice him out:

> Mallory would look into his room, soon after two o'clock, and find him plunged into a sort of melancholy stupor after the effect of a morning's teaching.
> 'Shall we go out?'
> 'No, I think I won't go out this afternoon – you don't mind do you? I shall go out a little later. Besides I am not fit company for the young and gay.'
> 'What nonsense: besides it is our regular day for going out – and I want to talk to you particularly. I have got stuck in an essay, and can't turn the corner.'
> 'Very well!' rising with an air of sullen resignation.
> 'Oh don't come if you really don't feel up to it – but you always get better out walking, you know.'
> 'Well, you mustn't let me talk about myself.'
> 'You won't have the chance – I have half a dozen things to tell you. You are the only person who really appreciates my experiences.'
> With such a graceful turn he would present the coming walk as a concession to himself and lift, so to speak, the lead of egoism from the invalid by exhibiting it upon his own shoulders.

After one such outing, Benson recorded in his diary:

It has been a quite perfect and delightful day. [...] One does not often get
the society of an ingenuous and congenial young man, who is also sincerely
affectionate, to oneself. [...] It has beguiled my depression in these gloomy
days as nothing else could have done.

But the most significant event of this last year at Cambridge was
the occasion when George first made the acquaintance of Geoffrey
Winthrop Young, the man who was to become his closest friend and
adviser, and who was to exercise such a strong influence on him for
the rest of his life. Geoffrey Young, now aged thirty-two, had been
educated at Marlborough and Trinity College, and while at Cambridge
had twice won the Chancellor's Medal for English Verse. After graduat-
ing in 1898 he had spent five years as a master at Eton and was now
an inspector of secondary schools. He was one of the finest British
mountaineers with an outstanding reputation in the Alps, where he
had put up many new routes in company with the Swiss guide Josef
Knubel. He was also well-known for his North Wales house parties, at
which a galaxy of mountaineering talent assembled every year at the
Gorphwysfa Hotel, at Pen y Pass at the foot of Snowdon.

George first met Geoffrey Young in February 1909, at a dinner in
Cambridge held in honour of the writer and critic Charles Lamb, to
which George had been invited by Charles Sayle. It was a very impressive affair with many eminent Cambridge notables present, including
the senior surgeon at Addenbrooke's Hospital, the Chief Secretary for
Ireland, the Regius Professor of Medicine, the Regius Professor of
Greek, the Professor of Sanskrit and the Professor of Chinese. George
found himself at a side table, sitting opposite Geoffrey Young, Maynard
Keynes and Rupert Brooke. It might have been an uneasy encounter,
for in the previous December George's old Winchester mentor, Graham
Irving, had read a paper to the Alpine Club describing his alpine climbs
with his 'recruits', as he termed his young Winchester companions. this
paper had caused a lot of dissent at the club. Many members considered
that he was endangering the lives of these young people by climbing
without the services of professional guides. Geoffrey Young had been
among thirteen other eminent members to sign a document expressing their disapproval. In the event, however, this first meeting was an

entirely happy occasion, and as Young later recalled: 'We became best friends at once. I invited him to Wales.' George was thrilled with the invitation, and on 19 February he wrote to Young:

> I am looking forward with unmixed delight to Easter, though I don't expect
> to fulfil your sanguine expectations. If by chance we may prove that one of
> the more terrifying places is less difficult than it looks, I shall leap for joy.

He need not have worried. He swiftly established his reputation and, in the Pen y Pass visitors' book, Young recorded that it was on this visit that George invented the Slab climb on the East Buttress of Lliwedd. Apparently his party had finished climbing for the day and were on their way home when George discovered that he had left his pipe on a ledge half-way up the face, where they had stopped for lunch. When later he rejoined his companions it transpired that, alone and in failing light, he had invented a new way to reach the ledge up a steep and exposed slab. On George's return to Cambridge Young sent him an application form for membership of the Climbers' Club. George wrote to thank him:

> Thank you for sending the Climbers' Club form. [...] I hope I shall be
> elected. Will you be there? If so you will be able to say if any question is
> asked that I was quite serious in offering the Traverse of the Malvern Hills
> as a qualification for the Club. You will agree that an expedition of that sort
> is only undertaken by people who care about the mountains – the right
> people that is for any club of mountaineers.

George was elected a member in May and soon afterwards he received an invitation from Geoffrey Young to join him in the Alps after his Cambridge term had finished.

As the summer of 1909 drew on, George gave a lot of thought to the question of his future career. He was interested in writing, but could hardly hope to earn a living by this means. At one time he had contemplated following in his father's footsteps and taking holy orders. Although he moved in intellectual circles which questioned traditional religious beliefs and was himself critical of what he considered to be the mere trappings of religion, he always professed to believe in the essentials of Christianity. In 1907 he had written to a Winchester friend, Edmund Morgan (later to become Bishop of Truro):

> For me, whatever else I may believe, the personality of Christ will live. [...] If all the facts of the Gospels were proved to be false, I should still believe that the figure of Christ was drawn in true characters and that the teaching of the Gospels is, in outline at all events, His teaching. That there is a God I have never doubted. That conviction seems to be a part of every feeling that I have.

He also served as Cambridge secretary of the Magdalene Lads' Club, the college mission in Camberwell, but, as he told Arthur Benson, he had misgivings about his suitability for the ordained ministry:

> I think it quite likely that I shall sometime become desperately keen on parish work of some kind; perhaps the only reason that I am not enthusiastic at present is that I'm at variance with so many parsons that I meet. They're excessively good, most of them, much better than I can ever hope to be; but their sense of goodness seems sometimes to displace their reason.

As time passed George began to consider the possibility of becoming a schoolmaster. In June he received a letter from his old headmaster, Dr Burge, which mentioned the possibility of a teaching post in mathematics, French and German at Winchester. But after visiting the school he realised that the job required too high a level of mathematical knowledge. And, as he told Geoffrey Keynes, he was also doubtful about his suitability to teach at Winchester:

> It sounds altogether rather too much as though the place were run according to fixed principles with many of which I should not agree. But then it is probably the same everywhere; I expect one will have to fight some battles.

His ideas were still undeveloped when he finally went down from Cambridge in July 1909. He had recently received a small legacy and he decided to spend some months in France to improve his knowledge of the language. But first there was that Alpine holiday with Geoffrey Young.

THREE

INTERIM 1909-1910

Geoffrey Young had planned a fortnight of guideless climbing. Setting out from Bel Alp, he and George climbed the Unterbächen on 1 August and were then joined by Donald Robertson, a friend of Geoffrey's. They had planned to make the first ascent of the south-east ridge of the Nesthorn, but bad weather drove them back to Bel Alp. On 4 August they set out again at 3 a.m., determined to have some activity, and tramped for three hours through rain, hail and snow. Then the weather improved and on a sudden impulse they decided to make their way up the Unterbächen again. As they basked in the sunshine on the summit they saw before them the long, unclimbed ridge leading to the Nesthorn. The prospect proved irresistible and they set out at once. By midday they had passed the highest point of the ridge and had started to climb the south-east arête. Soon after 4 p.m. they found themselves at the foot of the final obstacle – a conspicuous tower on the skyline.

Young reconnoitred the tower cautiously and noted that it might be possible to ascend by a very steep snow wall, but after ten hours in the lead he was reluctant to make the effort required. George thought that a route was possible up the south face. Young had great confidence in his ability:

> The effortless ease with which he wound up rocks which reduced me to convulsive struggling gave me reason to hope that he might be right. It was

for emergencies such as this that the younger and more brilliant cragsman
of the party had been so far, somewhat selfishly, kept in reserve.

They changed places on the rope and George began making his way
up a vertical slab and past an overhang. Young described what happened next:

> So far as I could see, he had no real holds at all; but he fought his way up
> magnificently, until all that remained below the rock cornice, which cut off
> everything else above from my sight, was his two boots. They were clinging,
> cat-like, and continued to cling for long seconds, to almost imperceptible
> irregularities on the walls of the rift. The mere sight of them made me breath-
> less; and I tightened every muscle, ready to spring the rope on its nick. For, on
> such foot-holds no climber would choose to wait long, were his hand-holds
> adequate for a lift; and if George's hand-holds were not adequate – ! Anyway,
> they did not serve for the gymnastic backward swing, outward and upward,
> which he was forced to risk. I saw the boots flash from the wall without even
> a scrape; and equally soundlessly, a grey streak flickered downward, and past
> me, and out of sight. So much did the wall, to which he had clung so long,
> overhang that from the instant he lost hold he touched nothing until the rope
> stopped him in mid-air over the glacier.

Wryly reflecting that the Austrian rope which they were using that
year had since been entirely condemned for its weak breaking strain,
Young later commented:

> I suppose two rather abnormally resilient anatomies at either end of a rope
> may introduce a confusing element into the nicest theory of strains.

George was unhurt. Apparently unperturbed, he rapidly climbed back
up the cliff and rejoined Young who was impressed by the fact that he
had not even let go of his axe during his fall. The whole incident had
passed so swiftly that the third member of the party, 20ft below and
round the corner on the north face, was totally unaware that anything
was amiss. With a great effort, Young now managed to climb the steep
snow wall that he had rejected earlier and they regained the ridge.

Speed was now essential and George was again sent into the lead. He made very swift progress. As Young observed:

> He appeared, through the shadows, to float like a thistle-down up the last abrupt steps. Now and again my eye was half-caught by a splash of light like an aureole that came and went over his stir of shadow moving above me. And then I saw that this was George's long hair, roughed out by the wind and catching or losing as he climbed [...] the last sunlight lifting above the ridge.

They reached the summit of the Nesthorn at seven o'clock and were rewarded by the most glorious sunset that George had ever seen. But there was no time for delay and they did not even stop to eat. They raced down the north arête and darkness had fallen by the time they began the trudge down the Ober Aletsch glacier. They reached the hotel at Bel Alp just after midnight: they had been out for 21 hours.

Three days later they tackled the south-east arête of the Finsteraarhorn. It was a long ascent, the climbing was hard and, when at last they gained the summit, the cold was positively numbing. George took the lead down the northern crest, cutting minute footholds down the steep ice-glazed slabs. Young, who was descending last, suddenly noticed that George had not reroped properly on leaving the summit, and that the rope between him and Robertson had become untied and was lying on a rock behind him. His reaction was one of considerable alarm:

> George looked to me so precariously placed that I was afraid of startling him into turning round by shouting to him what had happened. So I crooned to him urgently not to stir, and hissed direction to Donald to climb down and re-attach his rope. How do these things happen? Anyway, Donald from over-anxiety slipped out as he moved, the clatter of feet down the slab immediately behind him startled George in earnest; and as I saw him spin round like a flash on his one-foot ice-nick – well – what is it that one does feel at such seconds? What ever it is, I felt it, all of it, as I stared down the falling curve of icy slab, over the little fluster of figures, to the glacier five thousand feet below. My panic was unnecessary because the reassurance of a rope never meant anything to Mallory, who was as sure-footed and agile in recovery as the proverbial chamois.

After this incident the party continued carefully down the long and tiring descent.

Two days later they climbed the Jungfrau and then crossed to Chamonix where they were joined by the guide Josef Knubel. On 13 August they traversed the Aiguille Verte, descending by the Moine ridge. Bad weather then set in and, despite several attempts, they had to abandon a plan to make the first ascent to the Col des Nantillons. A few days later the weather relented and on a cloudless day they made a traverse of the Aiguille du Chardonnet. Young and Mallory then set out for Zermatt.

A young lady climber, Miss Cottie Sanders, who was in Zermatt that year, later recorded her impressions of meeting George for the first time:

> At the end of August 1909, a young man was sitting on an iron chair before a round iron table in front of the Monte Rosa Hotel at Zermatt, reading Galsworthy's *The Country House* in a Tauchnitz edition. Around him the tide of plans and gossip and guides and climbers – the whole *va et vient* of a summer's day at Zermatt – ebbed and flowed; but he sat in a sort of oblivion, never looking up, only sometimes raising a hand to push back the shock of brown hair which fell constantly over his forehead. He was picturesque and untidy, in loose grey flannels with a bright handkerchief round his neck; but the things which chiefly aroused attention were his good looks and his complexion. It was a bad season, with a good deal of new snow, and faces hideously disfigured by sunburn were the rule. But his young man's skin was clear and fair as a girl's. Presently another man came out of the hotel and roused him for an introduction. He got up at once, and went through it adequately, but with a sort of restive shyness, carefully controlled; the moment that courtesy permitted, he relapsed into his iron chair and his book. This was George Mallory and the man who was with him was Geoffrey Young.

Cottie Sanders soon struck up a friendship with George. She found him a charming and intriguing personality:

> He was very vague and ramshackly about everything practical. We travelled down to Visp with them when they left, and derived great amusement from

Geoffrey Young's efforts to get George packed and breakfasted and off in time. They galloped to the bus at the last second. When we got to Visp, George was sent to buy food while Geoffrey saw to the luggage. I met him in the restaurant, on the same errand. Something made him notice my alarm watch; he had not seen one before. 'Work it!' he said in his eager way. So we sat down at the table to make it work. Food and time were at once forgotten; and when the express came roaring in, nothing had been bought but a packet of Basler Leckerli, which I had got before I met him. We went out to the train; but he was still chiefly concerned to press on me the importance of going to Wales in September, and the value of Peck's Hardening Lotion for the feet. He gave us Peck's address – by which we guessed that he was, or had been at Cambridge – but not his own, though there was a loan of books or maps to be returned to him. And should we be at Zermatt next year? Because –. But the train bore them off; and the last we saw of him was his vivid face framed in the darkness of the carriage window, calling out something about a mountain.

Shortly after returning to England, George suffered an accident while climbing with some friends on a sandstone cliff in a disused quarry. It was three months before he shamefacedly described the incident to Geoffrey Young:

I would have written you a letter long ago only it involved a humble confession! About three weeks after we came back from Switzerland I had a nasty fall while climbing on a little sandstone cliff in Birkenhead and sprained an ankle – which has caused much trouble, for the said ankle refused for a long time to get any better and I hobbled about shamefully – indeed it is still in a poor state and though I am well enough for a short distance it is no good for the mountains. However, it seems certain now that it will get quite strong again and I actually climb a little on a quarry nearby and so I dare write. The whole affair is almost too disgusting to think of – a result chiefly of my obstinacy. I had been climbing about for some time with some friends when I suggested a possible new route; one of the other people who had never climbed before that day jeered greatly at the idea; so of course I was obliged to make the attempt at once. I like to think that I should have turned back if I hadn't been encouraged by a rope which was let down from above because my situation looked perilous. But at all events I went up on a hold which I knew to be unsafe, persuading myself that if the worse were to happen I could save myself with the rope; I deceived myself of course and when I slipped I grabbed at the rope but couldn't grip it tight enough.

In October, still unsure of his future career, George set out for an extended stay in France. After a short time in Paris, where he enquired at the Sorbonne about the possibility of obtaining some teaching work in the following year, he travelled south to the Alpes Maritimes to stay with the Bussy family. Simon Bussy was an artist and an acquaintance of Renoir, and his wife Dorothy was a sister of George's Cambridge friend, James Strachey. George had met the Bussys in Cambridge and had been invited to spend the winter with them at their villa in Roquebrune. Although he missed the old life in Cambridge, George took pleasure in his new surroundings. As he told Geoffrey Young:

> Roquebrune is a charming village built on a hillside and Italian in all but the fact that it is in France. It is halfway between Monte Carlo and Menton. [...] La Soucs is a small villa and it is a curious ménage. M. Bussy is a painter of some distinction and his wife is an elegant English lady; both are very intelligent and highly cultured people and at the same time unaffected, simple and even domestic – a good combination to live with. They have one little daughter.
>
> We all live for the most part on a large balcony which lies between the front door and the garden – a form of existence common enough I expect out here, but it is new to me and I find it charming. Higher up there is another balcony; I retire to this when I wish to be solitary and look out over the sea to Monte Carlo, which looks well enough in the hollow under a bold headland.

In a letter to his sister Avie he wrote: 'My bedroom is about the size of a grand piano' and added:

> I think I have made a good impression by kissing the little girl; it was she however who made the advances.

George bathed in the Mediterranean most days and, as his ankle improved, he went for walks in the hills. He devoted much of his time to improving his knowledge of French. As he reported:

> I read, write, translate and even speak French with great energy. The conversations are apt to become mere fusillades since the sounds which I emit, being both vehement and discontinuous, are rarely intelligible to anyone but myself.

It was during this stay that Simon Bussy painted the portrait of George which is now in the National Portrait Gallery.

George left Roquebrune at the end of February 1910 and, after a short visit to Italy, where he visited Milan, Genoa, Pisa and Florence, he went to Paris where he rented a room near the Jardin de Luxembourg in the Rue Gay Lussac. He stayed a month in the city, attending lectures at the Sorbonne and engaging in French conversation whenever possible. He wrote home describing his activities:

> It is a curious life: a poky little room over a large street, lonely strolls in the Tuileries or the Jardin de Luxembourg which is nearby, and visits to the museums and other sights and sounds. I know very few people here at present. The man I see most of is a poet and literary critic and is very interesting on these subjects. [...] Unfortunately my friend is blind.
>
> The term at the Sorbonne has just begun and I attended a lecture today. I expect I shall go to a good many as there are interesting men there, and it improves one's French to hear it spoken in that kind of way.

On his return to England George faced up to the need to make a decision over his future career. He was still interested in teaching and for some weeks he took a temporary appointment at the Royal Naval College, Dartmouth. He enjoyed this experience greatly, writing to a friend:

> This charming experiment is to end in a day or two. Lord! how pleasant it has been! I have even learnt to enjoy my 'Early Schools' – five in a week! and out of bed at 6.15 punctually. I expect I have been a failure: it

is almost impossible to be serious with youth. But it does everyone good to be merry.

And he added facetiously :

The corpse of King Edward is to be interred today. [...] My feeling of gratitude to our late monarch is sadly dependent upon the fact that I have a whole holiday.

George went on to have interviews at several schools, including Haileybury, where his brother Trafford was a pupil. In June he paid a brief visit to Mobberley for the wedding of his sister Avie, and then went on to Pen y Pass with a Cambridge friend, Edward Evans. The weather was atrocious and they only managed one day's climbing, on Lliwedd. From Wales George went to the Lake District to see his old tutor Arthur Benson, who was taking a holiday at Loweswater. They managed to do several long walks together, including the ascent of Pillar. Benson later commented: 'I never saw anyone show such ecstatic delight as George in the presence of mountains.' And when George stripped off to bathe in Crummock Water, Benson described him as a 'fine figure, taking headers and racing in the sun'.

No definite job had emerged by the first week in July, when George received a letter from Gerald Rendall, the headmaster of Charterhouse, near Godalming in Surrey, and a cousin of Montague Rendall, George's mentor at Winchester, offering him a probationary appointment at £270 a year:

The work will be mainly or wholly on the Modern side. I cannot foresee the exact distribution of history, French, Latin and maths, but I shall do my best to accommodate these to your own preferences, and hope that it may be possible to place in your hands some at least of the higher teaching of history candidates preparing for scholarships.

With his future settled, George wrote to Geoffrey Young to secure his assistance in obtaining a temporary post for the month of August:

I have heard of a rather pleasant sounding job – to take a boy to the Alps in
August and make him climb – and wonder if you could write a few lines
which would help me to get it. It isn't very clear to me that I am the ideal
person for the situation, but I think I might behave with discretion if I was
made responsible in this way. However if you think I should endanger the
boy's life, I won't attempt to go – but if by chance you think otherwise – then I
should be very grateful if you would again employ your pen in my service.

Young willingly obliged and in August George found himself escort-
ing fifteen-year-old John Bankes-Price to Switzerland. His parents
wished their son to have an introduction to Alpine climbing, a task
which George described as 'bear-leading'.

In the event, this time proved a period of acute frustration for
George, because the boy showed little inclination for any energetic
activity. They began at Bel Alp and George reported:

We pitched the tent for two days above the snow very successfully, but
afterwards my pupil hurt a knee, and we've had a very slack time in consequence.

After spending a week at Bel Alp they travelled to Zermatt. Several
of George's friends were there including Geoffrey Young, who had
just done noteworthy ascents of the Dent d'Hérens and the Dent
Blanche, and Cottie Sanders, who was accompanied by her mother.
Cottie noted that John Bankes-Price could hardly have been a less
suitable pupil:

He had no taste whatever for the pursuit; he was weak and clumsy, he
disliked cold and heat and exertions, and it was impossible to kindle in him
the smallest spark of enthusiasm.

His friends admired George for discharging his responsibilities
towards his pupil so conscientiously, continually urging him on, joking
with him and never openly losing his patience. Once he left John in
the care of Cottie Sanders, while he dashed off to make what proved
to be an unsuccessful attempt on the Arbegrat, one of the ridges of

the Weisshorn. But he continued in his efforts to encourage John and managed to get him to make ascents of the Trifthorn and the Riffelhorn. After a week at Zermatt they moved on to Arolla where they completed a traverse of Mont Collon. George obviously had some beneficial influence on the boy, who wrote to him two months later saying that he had never enjoyed a holiday so much and that he intended to go climbing whenever he could. George for his part had learned something about patience. He was going to need this quality a great deal more in his new life as a schoolteacher.

FOUR

SCHOOLMASTER:
CHARTERHOUSE 1910-1914

Charterhouse was founded in 1611 by Thomas Sutton, a Lincolnshire man, who had made his fortune in coal. The school was originally established at Clerkenwell in the City of London, on the site of an earlier Carthusian priory, and its foundation was intended to provide education for forty poor boys. Former pupils included Joseph Addison, John Wesley and William Makepeace Thackeray. In 1872 the decision was taken to move to Godalming in Surrey, where the school rapidly developed to become one of the most distinguished in the country.

George arrived at Charterhouse on 21 September 1910 at the start of the Michaelmas term and took up rooms with two colleagues in Nercwys House. The headmaster, Dr Gerald Rendall, was a kindly man who did not believe in iron discipline and had rather let things slide. It was not easy for a newcomer to settle in and George soon found that, despite his earlier impressions at Dartmouth, the role of schoolmaster was not an easy one to fulfil. Nonetheless, a few days after his arrival, he wrote cheerfully enough to his mother:

> I am enjoying life here, though there are moments of doubt. My work is a good deal with small boys, who are much more difficult to teach and to control; but it amuses me, and that is the great thing. Dreariness is fatal to success in teaching, and if I escape that I may learn to be of some use.

One of his problems was his absurdly youthful appearance. He was repeatedly taken by parents as one of the boys in the school. He also tended in his teaching to rely on infectious enthusiasm rather then on imposing his authority. He tried to discuss questions with his pupils in the open way that he had done with his friends at Cambridge, and he was not helped by his fast, rather nervous style of speaking. He recommended them to read widely and he set essays on such discursive topics as Popularity, Candour and Hypocrisy. He also took boys on expeditions to places of scenic beauty or of architectural importance. But some boys took advantage of this approach and at first he had many difficulties. He did not keep very good order and, as David Pye later reported:

> He used to relate with great satisfaction the tale of how the headmaster, passing his classroom door one day and hearing unaccustomed sounds from within entered to find the class acting the part of the crowd in Julius Caesar, which they were then reading, with the greatest realism and enjoyment.

Many of the staff became hostile towards him because of his informal approach, considering that it undermined their own attempts to maintain discipline. This situation was not helped by his readiness to criticise many public school conventions which he felt to be stultifying, nor by his lack of interest in the traditional sporting activities of the school. A revealing insight into his position is given by the writer Robert Graves, who was then a pupil:

> The most important thing that happened in my last two years [...] was that I got to know George Mallory: a twenty-six or twenty-seven-year-old master, not long up from Cambridge and so youthful looking as to be often mistaken for a member of the school. From the first he treated me as an equal, and I used to spend my spare time reading in his room, or going for walks with him in the country. He told me of the existence of modern authors. My father being two generations older than myself and my only link with books, I had never heard of people like Shaw, Samuel Butler, Rupert Brooke, Wells, Flecker, or Masefield, and the discovery excited me.
> He tried to treat his class in a friendly way, which puzzled and offended them, because of the school tradition of concealed warfare between boys

and masters. [...] Yet he always managed to find four or five boys who were, like him, out of their element, befriending and making life tolerable for them.

Another impression is given by a boy called Martineau, who was at the school between 1910 and 1914:

He was a handsome and popular young man, too easily amused to keep strict order, but one day, when I stank out a neighbouring Form by pouring ink on calcium carbide through the dividing door, he seized a fragment of broken desk, bade me bend over, and left a strong impression of muscularity on my hindquarters.

Mr R.L. Arrowsmith, one of his pupils who later became a housemaster at the school, felt that George was not a great success as a teacher, commenting, 'his heart was not in it'. And George's climbing friend, Cottie Sanders, who often visited him at Charterhouse, later wrote:

He was [...] working perhaps too much outside the ordinary scholastic framework of a public school to be a very successful schoolmaster, but he must have been a rather exciting one.

As the end of his first year of teaching approached, however, George began to feel a little more confident about his position. During the summer term he had developed the habit of camping out in the Surrey woods. As he told Cottie Sanders:

I'm grateful for the country − Lord; it is good about here − particularly as I spend many glorious nights under the stars. I expect I told you about the proposed site for my camp. It has been rather a success: my brother comes over from Guildford and one of the beaks [masters] from here. [...] A farm supplies bread and eggs and washes up our messes. A nightjar perches in the Scotch firs a few yards away and makes a thrilling music; the mist is white in the valleys; and there is no hill between our heathery crunch and Hindhead ten miles away. The sun gives the signal for our uprising (in theory) and one often gets an hour's work done before early school.

In a letter to his old tutor, Arthur Benson, he expressed mild satisfaction at his progress:

> Things go fairly well here, but it is very uphill work, and there are a good many horrors when one sees people getting visibly worse through being at school. However, this last term has been very agreeable; several things got better. I got less irritable and found it easier to be severe without being angry. Also the other ushers [teachers] seemed to be more friendly. There is only one common task I really dislike. Imagine me tomorrow morning teaching the smallest boys about the fall of man! What the devil is one to say?

In September 1911 Dr Rendall was succeeded as headmaster by Mr Frank Fletcher. Fletcher came from the headmastership of Marlborough, where he had earned a reputation for toughness, and under his leadership standards at Charterhouse steadily improved. But at first George was not very happy under the new regime. He took a personal dislike to Fletcher, whom he compared to a whale with the comment: 'He often looks as though he were trying to vomit the prophet Jonah.' It was only later that he came to recognise some of Frank Fletcher's virtues.

During Michaelmas term 1911 George devoted considerable time to revisiting his Cambridge essay on Boswell which Arthur Benson had suggested he should submit for publication as a book. He sent the manuscript to the publisher John Murray, who said that although his work was 'creditable and careful' he did not feel able to publish it. Undeterred by this refusal, George sent the manuscript to a second publisher, Smith, Elder and Co. They replied saying that although they would like to publish the book it would be necessary for him to make a thorough revision of the text. George showed the letter to Lytton Strachey who was on a visit to Charterhouse at the time. Strachey agreed with Smith, Elder that the book needed revision and, after reading the text, he wrote to George:

> I think you seem to be rather anxious to include too much, both in the sentences and in the general scheme. A good many of the sentences appear to me to be overloaded. I think it is usually better to sacrifice

comprehensiveness to lucidity, especially in prose. One can only hope to
say a part of what one thinks, and so one may as well make up one's mind
to choose the part that's simple.

Boswell the Biographer was eventually published in October 1912.
Mallory explained in his preface that it was not intended as 'a complete
Life of Boswell, but an explanation of his character'. It received quite good
reviews. The *Oxford Chronicle* referred to it as 'a valuable footnote to the
literary history of the Eighteenth Century', while the *Contemporary Review*
called it 'a thought provoking and satisfying book' and observed:

> Mr Mallory deserves great credit for his painstaking researches into the life,
> or rather the character, of the great writer. His work, while unpretentious,
> is yet eminently interesting and thoroughly readable.

George was pleased to receive a letter of praise from Cottie Sanders
(who later became a successful novelist writing under the name of Ann
Bridge) and told her: 'I never imagined that anyone would care about
it except "Boswell students", so it's all the more pleasing to hear that
you like it.' And he added:

> My father (who is not a great reader) has apparently been reading my
> Boswell on Saturday afternoons instead of preparing sermons – I therefore
> consider it a great success!

But the book was not a commercial success. George's contract had
stated that he would not receive any royalties until the publishers had
recovered their costs, a point which would not be reached until 455
copies had been sold. A year later his publishers reported that only 207
copies of the 1,000 which they had printed had been sold, and so sales
had not 'reached a point affecting his percuniary interest', although
they added rather unctuously:

> We are anxious that you should not suppose that there is the slightest repin-
> ing on our part over the publication of your Work which we still think has
> deserved a better recognition than it has received from the public.

As he gained in experience, George began to derive greater enjoyment from his life as a schoolmaster. He was constantly seeking ways of improving his teaching and the understanding of his pupils. He took part in school debates, usually on the unpopular, radical side. In his own reading he was always looking for material which would be suitable for the boys, and he never lost his enthusiasm, although he once exclaimed in despair, 'How am I to read *Paradise Lost* with a form of 30 boys?' In the summer of 1913 he collaborated with Robert Graves and two other boys in bringing out a new school magazine called *The Green Chartreuse*. This was intended to be a rival to the rather staid official school magazine, *The Greyfriar*. It appeared on Old Carthusian Day and was advertised by a huge poster on the cricket pavilion, depicting a larger than life-sized monk dressed in vivid green quaffing an uplifted glass. This was the work of the artist Duncan Grant and, according to David Pye, it created 'some flutter among the decorous upholders of public school proprieties'. The magazine contained a perceptive article by Graves satirising the school's traditional customs and slang.

In the spring of 1914 George gave a series of lectures on Italian painting to the school. He reported his efforts to Geoffrey Young:

I sweated much to produce some lectures on Italian pictures and really I think in the end succeeded. I gave three formal lectures [...] about Botticelli, Raphael & Michelangelo – much talk about paintings never seen by me & a good lot of general jaw meant to be somewhat provocative; and three informal shows: and in the end about 20 boys seemed really interested and keen to go on and take trouble to learn and think about it. Of course I didn't cater for any but the top parts of the school so I'm well pleased to get so many. [...] Some good fun with my form too in an odd hour – a sort of debate with plenty of discussion of a rather philosophical nature, 'that happiness is independent of pleasure' and such like themes; one great discussion 'That the majority of men get worse as they grow older' – imagine the irony in discussing that with boys!

He was also delighted when the artist Duncan Grant agreed to paint two pictures for his classroom.

Although naturally reserved, George made great efforts to get to know the boys in out-of-school hours, and he regularly held play-readings for

them in his room at Nercwys House. Cottie Sanders, who frequently
visited him at the school, described the scene:

> Friends visiting him at Charterhouse in the little house which he shared
> with one or two other masters, found the room a litter of books and papers
> – books in French and English, modern plays which were being examined
> with a view to readings with his brighter spirits, Fabian tracts, reproductions
> or photographs of Greek sculpture or modern French paintings – all more
> or less downed in a sea of essays from his form.

In the early months of 1914 George struck up a close friendship
with the Turner family, who lived at Westbrook near Godalming. Hugh
Turner was an architect whose wife had died in 1907, leaving him
with three teenage daughters to bring up. George first met the family
when he acted in a play in which the daughters also had parts, and
he became a regular visitor to their home, to play billiards with Mr
Turner or to go out walking. Westbrook had been built by Hugh
Turner in a magnificent setting on a hill dominating Godalming with
a view over the Wey valley towards Charterhouse. In March 1914
the family invited George to join them on a holiday in Italy. He had
already planned a walking holiday in the Apennines and readily agreed.
He met them in Verona at the begining of April, and they spent the
following week in Venice, during which he rapidly fell in love with
Hugh Turner's second daughter Ruth. They became engaged on May
Day. George wrote to his mother:

> I'm engaged to be married. What bliss! And what a revolution! Ruth
> Turner – she lives just over the river from here in a lovely house and with
> lovely people, and she's as good as gold, and brave and true and sweet.
> What more can I say! I fixed it up this morning. It was with Ruth and
> her family that I was staying in Venice, and it was there my own mind
> became resolved.

And he expressed his feelings to Cottie Sanders (now married to
Owen O'Malley):

Oh! dear! I am happy – and in what a strange and unexpected way! I'm glad you recommended married life. It'll be a furious revolution for me – and all the better for that.

George's brother Trafford (now in his final year at Magdalene College) wrote to express his delight:

This is good news indeed. I am very pleased to hear it; heartiest congratulations! I must say that I was extraordinarily surprised. However I suppose the influence of spring and Italy, combined with meeting the right person, fairly laid you by the heels.

On hearing of their engagement, an aunt of Ruth Turner's wrote to Cottie Sanders, not knowing that she knew George:

My niece, Ruth Turner, is engaged to be married. She is [...] a soul of the most crystal wisdom, simplicity, and goodness – pure gold all through. She is going to marry a young Charterhouse master, George Mallory – I hope he is good enough for her, but it is hardly possible.

Cottie replied saying that George was one of the rarest spirits of his generation, and that it sounded as if she might be nearly good enough for him.

The couple seemed ideally matched. They both loved the beauty of the countryside and shared a passion for flowers. While George was interested in politics and had read widely, Ruth had a fluent knowledge of French and Italian and a strong artistic sense, although she had an inherent weakness over spelling. All was not plain sailing for them, however. Hugh Turner was worried over George's financial prospects as a young schoolmaster and did not immediately give his consent to the marriage. Thinking it would be good for the two to be apart for a while, he took his daughters to Ireland on a fishing holiday for three weeks. George gave Ruth a copy of Edward Whymper's *Scrambles in the Alps* and they wrote to each other almost every day. On 15 May Ruth reported their arrival in Ireland:

My dearest we have got here. I have been looking for some time at the hill
I want to go up. I can't call it a mountain while I am reading *Scrambles in
the Alps*. It isn't very far off as the crow flies, but I shall have to go a long
way round a lake that lies along the foot of it. [...] I do wish you were here
and we could go off and explore the very wildest parts. We might go on
from place to place and stay a night or two away – but we will do that sort
of thing some time.

George replied:

If only I could walk those hills with you! But as you say, we shall; we shall
before so very long. It is good that you love the hills, and I'm glad you're
interested by Whymper's *Scrambles in the Alps*. The more I think of it, the
more convinced I become that we ought to have a proper climbing season
this year in the Alps.

After attending a reception at the headmaster's house George
reported that Mrs Fletcher had been asking questions about their
arrangements for the future:

Too many questions, I thought, but I suppose women can't help being
like that, however nice they are – e.g. what colours our rooms were to
be, black or purple or anything of that sort? A reference, I suppose, to my
Posty tastes.

He went on to suggest that they should have 'an emerald room and
a sapphire room and an amethyst room', to which Ruth replied that
she thought 'an Alpine' one would be more suitable for him. At last,
on 30 May, George was able to write:

Tomorrow and the day after tomorrow – and then! It's a short time before
Wednesday. Good night, Beloved.

At the end of June, George took Ruth to meet his parents in
Birkenhead. His father later wrote that the visit had left a very
pleasant impression: 'We like Ruth so much and it is delightful to see

you both so happy.' The wedding was held at Godalming on 29 July. George's father performed the ceremony and Geoffrey Young acted as best man. George had originally set his heart on a honeymoon in the Alps, but on informing Geoffrey Young of his intention he received a stern warning in reply:

> Now look here: if you mean by 'climbing' a respectable journey in a jolly district with decent passes and small excursions when found attractive – yes. But if you mean real climbing, in a big district, or long days for her – then absolutely no. You simply must put it out of your mind, for this year.
>
> Now – forgive my going on, but I feel this sincerely – your weakness, if any, is that you do let yourself get carried away on occasions in the mountains. [...] I think that it is your failing, the consequence of your combination of extraordinary physical brilliance in climbing and of power of mental absorption in it, that you do not, or at least have not, held back from allowing yourself to sweep weaker brethren, carried away by their belief in you, to take risks or exertions that they were not fit for, and which had the crisis come, neither you nor any man in climbing could have the margin to cover for both.

George hastened to reply that he had never intended to take Ruth on big expeditions:

> I had thought of the Oberland [...] with such peaks, as one might choose outside the biggest if one wished to make climbing attractive and not too arduous. [...] And in the second place I didn't propose to go at once to the Alps; we are going to have a really restful time at Porlock – a little place where Exmoor meets the sea, which sounds perfect – Ruth wants to sleep under the stars – do all the good things even more than I.

In the event, the outbreak of war on 4 August prevented any further discussion. After a short stay in North Somerset, George and Ruth enjoyed a camping holiday on the Sussex coast. In the feverish early days of the war this activity attracted attention and for a brief time they were held on the suspicion of being German spies.

FIVE

MOUNTAINEER 1910-1914

After taking up his teaching post at Charterhouse, mountaineering continued to play an important part in George's life. In December 1910 he was elected a member of the Alpine Club and a few days later he decided to attend the club reception at the Grafton Galleries. Cottie Sanders, who had invited him to tea beforehand, noticed that with typical absent-mindedness he had no idea of the formal dress required for the occasion:

> He came up fully purposed to go to an evening reception of about a thousand people in a very nice, old, comfortable greenish tweed suit and the very odd-looking porridge-coloured felt hat which was then his favourite headgear. It never occurred to him to bring any evening clothes. He explained to me afterwards that it was, after all, an Alpine Club reception – a gathering of climbers! so who *could* have presupposed evening dress?
>
> I was taking a party to the Ladies A.C. for dinner and had to go off to dress. I don't know who it was that enlightened George in the matter of the dress suit; but when I came down I learned that he had been enlightened, had been filled with dismay, had rumpled his hair – and fled.

George spent the new year of 1911 in North Wales, at Pen y Pass. Cottie Sanders, who was also there with her brother Jack, never forgot her first outing on that occasion. She was suffering from muscular strains and had also caught a chill:

I felt very unlike doing anything, but consented to walk up to Lliwedd with Geoffrey and George to see them start. I had my first experience that day of a certain inexorableness there was in George if he thought one ought to climb – and Geoffrey was worse. 'The rocks look bone dry today, Mallory. I think we ought to have a very pleasant day, Miss Sanders, if you feel inspired to it when you get there.' But I didn't, and said so – and that I would watch them climb. It was no use. They were full of consideration. 'But you must climb something, Miss Sanders,' from Geoffrey. 'Something quite short, of course,' from George. Then both: 'Seriously, it isn't any particular pleasure to either of us to do one of these things together again. We'll do something with you; we don't mind a slack day.' The slack day resolved itself, I found, into the Girdle Traverse when we were half-way up the Far East Buttress. But that was too much. I was bitterly cold and feeling rather ill and completely off climbing; in fact I was frightened out of my wits at being on rocks at all in such a state. I asked to be taken to the top. I was, by devious routes, but with a certain silence in front and behind. We lunched on the top; and Geoffrey went on up Snowdon, while George took me home in sad disgrace. He was kind, but a little mocking and inquisitive as to why I should have been so frightened – it clearly was something he had no experience of whatever. But when he saw that I was really unhappy over it he left off teasing and saw to it that I got a huge tea and afterwards offered to take me up to the little lake behind the hotel, which I had expressed my intention of seeing.

The next day George took Cottie and her brother Jack to climb the Central Buttress of Tryfan. Cottie later recalled: 'We were rather feeble creatures and his patience with us was extraordinary', and she remembered him 'moving about over the rocks like a great cat, scolding, exhorting, encouraging us'. She had a high regard for George's climbing abilities:

He was never a showy climber; he did not go for the minute precisions of style at all. On the contrary, he seemed to move on rocks with a sort of large, casual ease which was very deceptive when one came to try and follow him. When he was confronted with a pitch which taxed his powers, he would fling himself at it with a sort of angry energy, appearing to worry it as a terrier worries a rat, till he had mastered it.

Geoffrey Young also had a high regard for George's climbing style:

> He swung up rock with a long thigh, a lifted knee, and a ripple of irresist-
> ible movement. A perfect physique and a pursuing mind came together as
> it were in a singleness of power, as he rushed into motion.

At Easter that year George was back at Pen y Pass, a regular member
now of Geoffrey Young's famous house-parties. The Gorphwysfa
Hotel, under the proprietorship of Mr and Mrs Rawson Owen, was,
as Young later wrote, an admirable centre for their activities:

> With its 'beds and its brass', its artistic furniture and good cuisine, and later with
> its electric lighting and increasing supplies of hot bath-water, Gorphwysfa
> became a place of note. To be able [...] to return [...] there to bathe and gossip
> and sing and steam-bath carelessly and endlessly at the close of a strenuous
> day, while waiting for the roar of Mrs Owen's fandango on the dinner gong,
> made a social feature in the Welsh parties unique of its kind.

Immense care was taken in the selection of the party. Then it was left to
itself, and organisation reduced to a minimum. All plans had to be kept in
the background, about 'coming' and 'going' details. The party flashed into
being in full bright plumage; ran for a few days like the Golden Age, and
melted as silently and suddenly. After prodigious feats in the mountains
during the day, the long evenings were spent in impromptu songs and
varied entertainments, alternated with gymnastic exploits in the hall.

Many of those who came to the Pen y Pass house-parties were also
eminent in public life. Years later, in his book *On High Hills*, written
in 1927, Geoffrey Young commented:

> As I look through the list of names, three earned the Order of Merit,
> four had the Nobel Prize, five became cabinet ministers, seven were made
> peers and one a life peer, fifteen were knighted and of course an indefinite
> number became honorary doctors.

Out of all the talented climbers who gathered there over the years,
Geoffrey Young later selected three who stood out in his memory,

Hugh Pope, Siegfried Herford and George Mallory. Of Pope, who
died climbing in the Pyrenees in 1912, he wrote:

> Six foot four in statuesque height and an all-round athlete, he climbed with
> an indolent but fluent certainty and balance, and with an advantage of reach
> that devoured rock distances.

He said of Herford, who died fighting at Ypres in 1915, that:

> He was an originator. [...] His lead up the Flake Crack on Scafell is some-
> times cited as the beginning of the transition to modern methods and
> standards. It is probably the first recorded use of slings or stirrups as aids
> since Alexander the Great. An engineer, with a deep strain of poetry and
> romance, his style of rock climbing would have been at home among recent
> developments. From his knee to his shoulder there looked to be a single
> powerful spiral of muscle, which enabled him to straighten in balance on
> infinitesimal stances.

And of Mallory he wrote:

> He was the greatest in his fulfilled achievement; so original in his climbing
> that it never occurred to us to compare him with others or to judge his
> performance by ordinary mountaineering standards. Chivalrous, indomi-
> table, the splendid personification of youthful adventure; deer-like in
> grace and power of movement, self-reliant and yet self-effacing and radi-
> antly independent. On a day he might be with us; on the next gone like
> a bird on the wing over the summits, to explore some precipice between
> Snowdon and the sea; whence he would return after nightfall to discuss
> climbs or metaphysics in a laughing contralto, or practise gymnastics after
> his hot bath, on the roof beam of the old shack, like the youngest of the
> company.

And years later, recalling a sun-soaked day spent climbing with George
on the Glyders from which they had returned under the light of the
moon, he observed:

> On a day like this, [...] Mallory was wholly in harmony within himself, and
> with the world, and nothing could give him pause.

One of the guests that Easter of 1911 was the Austrian climber,
Dr Karl Blodig, who had almost completed his ascents of all fifty-seven
Viertausender, the 4,000m peaks in the Alps, an outstanding feat that
he was to achieve a few months later. On 12 April, two parties started
the ascent of the Great Gully on Craig yr Isfa. Dr Blodig, who was
leading the first party, found himself confronted with an iced chimney
which caused him some misgivings:

> I favoured going back and finding another route, but that did not please
> the second party at all. Mr Mallory climbed up, turned his back against the
> block of ice, wedged himself in the chimney as best he could, and brought
> Mr Reade up. Then Mr Mallory used him as a human stepladder and with
> the greatest dash and marvellous skill, worked his way up the smooth surface
> until he disappeared from our view. Unanimous cries of 'Hurrah' and 'Bravo'
> hailed this extraordinary performance.

Three days later Mallory and Reade took Dr Blodig on the Girdle
Traverse of Lliwedd. Blodig later commented:

> Mr Mallory led; I brought up the rear. If I may venture to express an
> opinion, the coolness with which Mr Mallory showed his mastery of the
> hardest pitches was really outstanding – but then Mr Reade kept impressing
> on me from first to last the conviction that this man 'couldn't fall even if
> he wanted to'.

Despite this assurance, at the end of the day Blodig observed: 'That
man will not be alive for long'. Cottie Sanders noted how upset
George was at this comment:

> He always used to defend himself vigorously against any suggestion that he
> was not a perfectly prudent mountaineer and looked almost comically dis-
> mayed and surprised over this dictum. He was prudent, according to his own
> standards; but his standards were not those of the ordinary medium-good

rock-climber. The fact was that difficult rocks had become to him a perfectly normal element; his prodigious reach, his great strength, and his admirable technique, joined to a sort of cat-like agility, made him feel completely secure on rocks so difficult as to fill less competent climbers with a sense of hazardous enterprise. But he was very careful of unskilled performers, and very down on any clumsiness or carelessness. I never saw him do a reckless or ill-considered thing on steep rocks. He hated the irresponsible folly and ignorance which led incompetent people into dangerous situations and so brought mountaineering into disrepute.

On Easter Monday Mallory and Young, after a climb on Dinas Mot, turned aside to rescue a German who was in difficulties on the snowbound eastern wall of the Parson's Nose on Clogwyn y Person. Mallory was highly indignant when the man, who was dressed in ordinary shoes and a long mackintosh, offered his rescuers a sovereign. Cottie Sanders noted in her diary that evening:

> Doctor Blodig decorated George and Mr Young with huge circular orange-coloured paper medals, with 'for life safing [sic] on each'.

A vivid impression of George that year is given in Cottie Sanders' account of a long discussion in the smoking-room one damp evening:

> Owing to the death of someone's grandfather, the usual sing-song was not taking place; the old gentlemen were doing feats of strength with Geoffrey and Owen in the hall, and the younger members gathered rather *désoeuvrés* round the fire under Mrs Reade's presidency. George and one of the Irishmen were the protagonists and the subject was whether one should or should not have principles. George held that one should – at least one or two fundamental ones – and keep as close to them as possible. The Irishman had no objection to one's having principles, so long as he was prepared to break them. Mrs Reade pronounced herself to have none. Here were the makings of a famous ethical row – and we had it!
>
> The Irishman really had all the cards in his hands: he was quick, he was witty, his mind was rather deadly in its keenness, he was exceedingly well-informed

and he was taking the side easiest to defend – the broad-minded, airy, tolerant point of view. It was not difficult for him to make George's insistence on the importance of thinking right and doing right look pedestrian and priggish, and he was very unsparing. And the sense of the meeting was on the whole against George – at the start, anyhow. George stood up to it superbly, really: no irony, no dialectical skill, would budge him from his position – that it might and must be necessary to alter the letter of principles to suit fresh facts as they entered a person's experience, but that the spirit informing them would remain the same. There was a right, and if you wanted to you could find it, and it was supremely important. The discussion grew very heated. George was really outmatched; but the thing that gradually emerged most, for me, was the practical demonstration he was giving of living up to the principle of keeping one's temper in an argument – in spite of shrewd blows given and received. And his extraordinary insistence on purity of motive.

I have a picture of the group now: Mrs Reade on one side of the fire; the Irishman opposite, with his feet over the arm of his chair, mowing down opposed theories with the skill of a good fencer; George on the floor between them, his hands round his knees, unclasped now and then to throw back his hair, stammering a little with his eagerness and impatience and the difficulty of getting out what he had to say, but getting it out all the same; while in corners pairs expounded their views to one another or put in a quick word.

The beginning of August found George in the Alps once more, this time with his Winchester friends, Graham Irving and Harry Tyndale. Years later Tyndale recalled his impression of George leading on steep ice on the ascent of the north ridge of the Grivola:

> He cut a superb staircase, with inimitable ease and grace and a perfect economy of effort. In watching George at work one was conscious not so much of physical strength as of suppleness and balance; so rhythmical and harmonious was his progress in any steep place, above all on slabs, that his movements appeared almost serpentine in their smoothness.

Their main achievement that season was the ascent of Mont Blanc by the eastern buttress of Mont Maudit in a long day of sixteen and a half hours, during part of which George was affected by a stomach disorder brought on from drinking some sour Chianti the night before. He later wrote an essay for the *Alpine Journal* in which he reflected on his innermost feelings on reaching the summit of Mont Blanc:

> The solemn dome resting on those marvellous buttresses, fine and firm above all its chasms of ice, its towers and crags; a place where desires point and aspirations end; very, very high and lovely, long-suffering and wise. [...] *Experience*, slowly and wonderfully filtered; at the last a purged reminder. [...] And what is that? What more than the infinite knowledge that it is all worth while – all one strives for? [...] How to get the best of it all? One must conquer, achieve, get to the top; one must know the end to be convinced that one can win the end – to know there's no dream that mustn't be dared. [...] Is this the summit, crowning the day? How cool and quiet! We're not exultant; but delighted, joyful; soberly astonished. [...] Have we vanquished an enemy? None but ourselves. Have we gained success? That word means nothing here. Have we won a kingdom? No ... and yes. We have achieved an ultimate satisfaction ... fulfilled a destiny. [...] To struggle and understand – never this last without the other; such is the law.

Early in September, before returning for the Michaelmas term at Charterhouse, George went with his sister Mary to the Snowdon Ranger Inn at Llyn Cwellyn and enjoyed a week's climbing with Harold Porter. their most memorable experience was on a gloriously sunny day on Lliwedd, during which they climbed half a dozen routes at a fast speed and mostly unroped. Porter recorded in his diary that it was the most enjoyable day of rock-climbing he had ever experienced. He had found it exciting to climb to the high standard set by Mallory, who, he said, 'climbed with that miraculous ease and grace which I had already learnt to admire'.

Over Christmas 1911 George took his brother Trafford to Pen y Pass. It was a very large house-party, which Geoffrey Young later described as reaching a 'climax of climbing and sociability'. They spent Christmas Day on Tryfan, and one snowy night they roamed over Crib Goch looking for two lost climbers. When the missing pair returned at dawn, their host, Rawson Owen, galloped bareback up the track from Pen y Pass, blowing a horn to assure them that all was well. The highlight of the evening entertainment was an uproarious session at which the pianist played a continuous accompaniment for two and a half hours while the assembled company composed parodies to the tune of *Blow the Man Down*. Cottie Sanders, who spent a day with George prospecting for routes on Clogwyn y Person, later recalled him:

> Roaming about, generally unroped, seeking a way, pausing in that characteristic attitude, one hand almost stroking the rock, while his eye wandered up and down looking for clues and weighing possibilities, till he decided that something would 'go'.

George was back at Pen y Pass, again with Trafford, at Easter 1912. Geoffrey Young had travelled to Wales in his car, which rejoiced under the name 'Coventry Swift'. Since it was the only car in the hills at that time, Geoffrey, who had excellent night sight, took to driving it without lamps; this practice sometimes had unfortunate consequences. One evening after dinner he returned a cheerful group to the Pen y Gwyrd Hotel at the foot of the pass. As Geoffrey laconically remarked:

> I arrived to find Leslie Shadbolt gone from beside me. The pivot seat had tipped, at the famous corner – and shot him out unseen.

But luckily the missing passenger was quite unhurt and followed them down the road none the worse for his experience.

That summer George was again in the Alps, but the weather turned out to be the worst for many years. The highlight of this poor season was a new route up the Dent Blanche with Hugh Pope and Harold Porter in a climb of seventeen hours. A few days later Mallory and Pope were joined by Geoffrey Young and made a direct ascent of the south wall of the Tête du Lion. George led the climb for most of the way. Young commented:

> Mallory overwhelmed the first little over hand with wave-like ease. His movement in climbing was entirely his own. It contradicted all theory. He would set his foot high against any angle of smooth surface, fold his shoulder to his knee, and flow upward and upright again on an impetuous curve. Whatever may have happened unseen the while between him and the cliff, in the way of holds or mutual adjustments, the look, and indeed the result,

were always the same – a continuous undulating movement so rapid and powerful that one felt the rock must either yield, or disintegrate.

Hugh Pope then left to go to the Pyrenees, taking with him an ice axe which George had lent him. On returning to England, George received a letter from Hugh thanking him for his 'introduction to the Alps'. Sadly, a few days later news came of Pope's death while on a solo ascent of the Pic du Midi d'Ossau. George was very upset, telling Cottie Sanders, 'he was such a charming companion in the Alps this year'.

By now, appreciative of what Graham Irving had done for him as a schoolboy, George had started the custom of inviting boys from Charterhouse to join him in the mountains. At Easter 1913, after the usual house party at Pen y Pass, three boys stayed with him at the Snowdon Ranger Inn at Quellyn. One of them was Robert Graves, who after returning home wrote to George:

> I never remember enjoying myself so much as at Quellyn. It was an experience to me in dozens of ways. [...] The rafters of this house have been continually ringing to the strains of the enthusiastically adapted *Green Grow The Rushes O.*

In September he took another Charterhouse boy, Alan Goodfellow, for a long weekend in Wasdale. They climbed on Scafell, Pillar Rock and Great Gable. While on Gable, George struck out on a new line which brought them to a small ledge covered with bilberries. He then realised that they were in an awkward situation. It would be very difficult to reverse their route, but to go on meant undertaking an unprotected traverse, for their rope was not long enough to permit a belay. Alan Goodfellow later recalled:

> It must have been a very anxious moment for George, faced with the respon-sibility of an inexperienced schoolboy climber as his only companion; but he showed no trace of it and quietly suggested that we should eat all the bilberries before we went on. Then we effected the traverse unbelayed, with George leading the way and instructing me exactly where to put my hands and feet. He was quite the finest rock–climber I have ever seen, with a wonderful sense of balance.

George was back at Pen y Pass just after Christmas. This visit was notable for the first Double Girdle Traverse of Lliwedd which he achieved in company with Young and Herford. After completing the single traverse they dropped down to a promising level and then crossed the whole face once more. Years later Geoffrey Young could still recall his view of 'the agile figures in white sweaters, swinging, turning, belaying to a counterpoint of precision and force'.

In the spring of 1914 George wrote an article for the journal of the Climbers' Club, in which he expressed the aesthetic feelings which he experienced in mountaineering:

> Climbers who, like myself, take the high line have much to explain, and it is high time they set about it. Notoriously they endanger their lives. With what object? If only for some physical pleasure, to enjoy physical movements of the body and to experience the zest of emulation, then it is not worth while [...] The only defence for mountaineering puts it on a higher plane than mere physical sensation.

He went on to compare the activity of climbing to a musical experience:

> A day well spent in the Alps is like some great symphony. *Andante*, and *andantissimo* sometimes, is the first movement – the grim, sickening plod up the moraine. But how forgotten when the blue light of dawn flickers over the hard, clean snow! The new motif is ushered in, as it were, very gently on the lesser wind instruments, hautboys and flutes, remote but melodious and infinitely hopeful, caught by the violins in the growing light, and torn out by all the bows with quivering chords as the summits, one by one, are enmeshed in the gold web of day, till at last the whole band, in triumphant accord, has seized the air and romps in magnificent frolic, because you are at last marching, all a tingle with warm blood, under the sun. [...] And so throughout the day successive moods induce the symphonic whole. [...] Mountaineers [...] claim that something sublime is the essence of mountaineering. They can compare the call of the hills to the melody of wonderful music, and the comparison is not ridiculous.

1 The Revd Herbert Leigh Mallory, George's father.

2 George's mother, Annie.

3 George with his sisters Avie and Mary.

4 Mobberley parish church, about 1900.

The College,
Winchester,
Sept 22/0

My dear Mother,

I'm sorry I didn't write to you before. I came here all right on Wednesday, alright, although by the 4 o'clock train instead of the 5.10, as otherwise I should have to have waited an hour at Waterloo which I didn't exactly relish. I found Mr Rendall, who took

me up to the Warden, who admitted me to College, and afterwards gave me tea.

I had a ripping time down at Sydenham; we went to the Crystal Palace, the Zoo & Hippodrome, all of which I enjoyed very much.

I like being here very much — ever so much better than Grengorse, & I like the men better too. (& instead of chaps we always say men): We have plenty of work to do, and I'm afraid I'm running

you up a heavy book bill; we shall begin playing foster — the Winchester game — for some time yet; we get up at 6.15, and begin work — morning lines its called at 7.0.

With much love,

Ever Your loving son,

George.

5 – 6 George's first letter home from Winchester, 22 September 1900.

7 George with his dog Springer.

8 George as the centrepiece of a gymnastic display at Winchester.

The College,
Winchester.

July 3 /04

My dear Mother,

My hasty letter of
Friday evening forgot its most
important object I meant
to send you the photo. I have
had taken here; I think it is
very good on the whole: your
birthday present is a most
excellent one & I am very
pleased at being able to give my
photo. to a lot of people here
who wanted one

I am quite aware that cash
is very scarce just now, which
makes my expedition to Switzerland seem rather a nuisance. The
only expense will be the ticket
out there; I don't know how
much that will come to, but
I hope Gra will give me something towards that — by way of
a birthday present —; then too
the cost of keeping me at home for
the three weeks or whatever it is that
I am in Switzerland would amount
to something considerable, so that
if you reckon the cost of the expedition

from that point of view it will come
to something very small I fancy.
The worst of my exam comes in
this week and I am not anti-
cipating any great joy there
from.

I suppose Mary has returned
home by now; it was rather
a pity she was not able to
stay longer on the second day
of Eton match.
With much love.
Yr. loving son,
George.

P.S. I am sending two different
photos; I daresay Father or
Mary might like one.

9 – 10 George's letter to his mother, 3 July 1904.

11 George with his sister Mary at a picnic by the River Dee.

12 *Above:* George with his sisters, Mary and Avie, Avie's fiancé Harry Longridge and Geoffrey Keynes.

13 *Right:* George with Arthur Benson outside Hinton Hall.

14 A family group at the silver wedding anniversary of George's parents, June 1907.

15 Magdalene College First VIII, 1908.

16 George (left) with his brother Trafford about to set out for a climbing holiday in North Wales, August 1908.

17 *Above:* George in his room at Cambridge during his last year, 1908/09.

18 *Left:* Geoffrey Winthrop Young.

19 *Opposite above:* George at Zermatt, August 1910.

20 *Opposite below:* George on the descent of the Moine Ridge, August 1909.

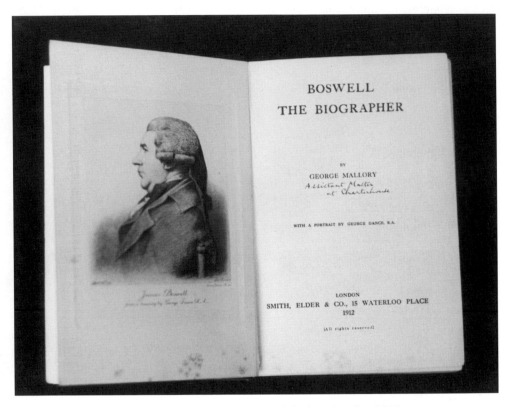

21 The title page of *Boswell the Biographer*, published in October 1912.

22 Ruth Mallory.

23 *Above:* A Pen y Pass group, 1909.

24 *Left:* George with Cottie Sanders and her brother Jack at Pen y Pass, Easter 1911.

25 *Above:* George (right) with Siegfried Herford at Pen y Pass, Christmas 1913.

26 *Right:* Second Lieutenant George Mallory.

27 George with his daughter Clare, 1917.

28 *Right:* Clare
and Beridge
Mallory, about
1920.

29 *Below:* George
at the wheel of
his car at Pen y
Pass, Easter 1919.

30 George sitting on the wall of the loggia at The Holt. The towers of
Charterhouse may be seen in the distance.

SIX

WAR 1914-1918

Before the start of the 1914 Michaelmas term, George and Ruth spent a week in the Lakes, staying at Row Head in Wasdale. Ruth was given a testing introduction to rock-climbing. Their programme included ascents of the Napes Needle and Kern Knotts Chimney on Great Gable, the New West Climb on Pillar Rock, and Jones's Pinnacle on Scafell. On returning to Charterhouse they took up residence in a rented house until their more permanent home should become available. The onset of war made normal life difficult. Ruth started work at the hospital at Godalming and, as his friends began to enlist, George became restive at his own comparatively comfortable life. His headmaster, Frank Fletcher, refused to release him from teaching. In November he expressed his frustration to Geoffrey Young who, after a short time as a war correspondent, had joined the Quaker ambulance unit in France:

> It becomes increasingly impossible to remain a comfortable schoolmaster – I read this morning the dismal tale of wet and cold, which makes my fireplace an intolerable reproach. Life jogs along pretty safe here. I lectured the other day to most of the school about the causes of the war – general talk about conflict of national characters, and about the Balkans, it was quite a great success and bucked me up; it's good to hear boys cheering oneself. Sometimes I go down to the hospital and hear the tommies' queer talk – very good folk most of them. What an experience of human beings you must be having!

At Christmas George introduced Ruth to the mountains of North Wales. They spent a fortnight at the Pen y Gwyrd Hotel climbing with George's Cambridge friend David Pye, who later described this visit as 'a most severe initiation: a time of gales and snowstorms, enough to daunt any but the stoutest-hearted novice'. He particularly remembered the occasion when, after climbing the Parson's Nose, they decided to go on over Crib y Ddysgl to the summit of Snowdon:

On the ridge the gale was of hurricane strength, screaming and whirl-ing the snow in all directions so that not a word was audible even when shouted in the ear. On our left was the snow slope down to Llyn Llydaw, and once over on that side there would be comparative shelter from the gale. But the slope in the driving snow and mist looked precipitously steep and terrifying. We were roped, Mallory in front, then his wife, myself last. When the wind at length became so fierce as to make breathing difficult and steady walking impossible Mallory decided that we must get down on to the sheltered side of the ridge. Explanations were impossible. I saw him point down the horribly steep looking slope and urge her in pantomime to take the plunge. From this, lacking our knowledge that it was in fact perfectly safe, she very naturally recoiled. And then there was enacted the most perfectly staged scene of mountaineering melodrama. Taking his wife by the shoulders, Mallory simply pushed her forcibly over the edge! I meanwhile, guessing what he was up to, stood down on the windward side to hold her rope. Next he jumped over also and soon we were all gasping in comparative peace while the wind still roared overhead.

At the end of December the Mallorys had to move out of their rented accommodation and they went to stay with Ruth's parents at Westbrook. This did not prove very convenient. As George later told Arthur Benson:

We lived cut off from Charterhouse by the river Wey; which generally made such big floods that I had a two-mile cycle ride to get to school; it sounds a small matter but you know the difference it would make in school life: I on one hill and the boys on another – there was a gulf fixed! And so I saw all too little of the boys. Nor was I completely happy to be living with my

George's letter to Cottie Sanders, 19 July 1915, discussing plans for a visit to Wales and mentioning Rupert Brooke's last volume of poems.

wife's people. They are very good people, but one doesn't want to live that way when one is married.

At last, in the spring of 1915, they moved into their new home, The Holt. This was an imposing house on the far side of the valley from Westbrook. It had been built in 1872 and had six bedrooms, an elegant dining room and a large airy sitting room which opened out on to a loggia, where one could sit out in comfort, shielded from the wind. The house had been bought for the couple by Ruth's father. At the end of May, George wrote to Geoffrey Young expressing his delight at his new home:

This is quite a charming little place. I spent most of yesterday sitting in our loggia – a place divinely sheltered from this keen north wind – just caught in the sun's warm comfort. It has a tiled floor and a low brick wall to lean your elbow on and support the posts that take the roof. The centre of our life, as you may imagine: the drawing room and dining room both give onto it. Below the house we have a strip of copse. The domain goes down far enough to provoke a question as to where it ends; it has a number of winding paths and certain flower beds carved out of the jungle – though the bottom is still practically unreclaimed copse and the proper wild spring flowers have been blooming all about – primroses, daffodils, celandines, bluebells, anemones. It is a steep warm bank and very green. Above it, a low terrace wall with the breadth of three tiles to sit on – guarding our little lawn and a small formal garden you go up steps to. And a glorious view of the Wey valley from everywhere.

Frank Fletcher persisted in his refusal to release George from teaching. In the previous December the War Minister, Lord Kitchener, had instructed headmasters to use their own judgement in deciding which of their staff might be permitted to enlist 'without impairing the work of these schools and the training of the OTC'. In March George wrote to his sister Avie expressing frustration at missing the chance to work in an anti-contraband department at the Admiralty:

> I did feel sick the other day. I was offered a commission by the Admiralty to help with the contraband business, under a friend – a most thrilling job, involving the commerce of all the world. Of course it wouldn't have been risking one's life, but it would have been wearing the King's uniform. I have an almost childish feeling for the virtue of that. However, there was no serious question of my being allowed to go.

In a letter to Arthur Benson, George expressed his dissatisfaction at his own comparatively easy life compared with the privations endured by some of his friends:

> It is true, I'm afraid, that I've been too lucky; there's something indecent, when so many friends have been enduring so many horrors, in just going on at one's job, quite happy and prosperous.

In May he made feelers to see if he might take a commission in the Flying Corps, only to receive a letter from Fletcher reiterating his refusal to let him go:

I was told the other day that you were 'going to take a commission in the
Flying Corps'. I certainly never gave my consent to this; I only agreed that
there would be no harm in your making enquiries, so that in case the War
Office asked us for more officers you might be ready among others. Till
they do [...] I cannot consent to your going.

Sensing his restlessness, Ruth, who was now expecting their
first child, encouraged him to spend part of the summer holidays
climbing in North Wales. He took with him Hugh Percy, a former
Charterhouse pupil, and at Pen y Pass he was joined by his climbing
friend, Cottie Sanders. She was now married to Owen O'Malley and
had reverted to her formal name of Mary Anne. They found that war
conditions prevailed even in North Wales. Soldiers were guarding
the pipeline from Llyn Llydaw to the neighbouring power station
and they were told they could not proceed. Nothing daunted, they
managed to dodge the sentries and went on to climb on Lliwedd.
George enjoyed this quiet period, climbing mainly standard routes
on Tryfan and Lliwedd. One day he rescued a small lamb on Tryfan
and brought it down to safety in his rucksack. He then went on
to spend three weeks on a cycling holiday with his father in the
Yorkshire Dales. The Mallorys' first child was born on 19 September,
a daughter whom they named Frances Clare. Writing to Mary Anne
O'Malley on 10 October George laconically observed:

I've told you nothing after all about the baby. – but what is there to say?
I suppose they all use the gestures of oratory & simulate a belief that the
world is at their feet? She increased 10 ozs this last week. And of course
she's sweet – so everyone says.

As news came of the deaths of some of his fiends, including Hugh
Wilson and Jack Sanders, Mary Anne's brother, George became
increasingly restive at his own position. He relieved his feelings by
composing a pamphlet entitled *War Work for Boys and Girls*, with the
aim of promoting ideas of international understanding. With Mary
Anne's help this pamphlet was published by Allen and Unwin in 1916.
It was an appeal to the youth of England to use their years at school

wisely, in order to prepare themselves to form an intelligent and well-informed public opinion. War not only set nation against nation and destroyed the lives of many good people, but also, by its appeal to the emotions and by the use of propaganda, it insidiously eroded the habit of clear thinking. Mallory exhorted the youth of England:

> Besides trying harder to live well and strenuously in your part of life, which is the first duty for all of us, you can think. We must think with all our minds, [...] think with imagination and sympathetically; think passionately and, not less, think calmly, without prejudice and critically – think and, when we think, devote ourselves to learning what is right for England.

At last the news came that the headmaster had found someone who could teach history in George's place, and he was free to go. One of his last acts at Charterhouse was to submit an article for the school magazine, *The Greyfriar*, on William Pitt the Elder, which later appeared in the April 1916 issue. George seems to have been influenced by his own situation and by the background of his own times when he wrote of Pitt:

> He was a great lover of his country. England knew his passion. Under the shadow of impending war she called for Pitt only and always for Pitt. His great ability she knew could only serve her interests. He was the incorruptible. To him, and to him alone in the age, she could come trusting; he had been proved single-hearted. [...] Therefore England came to him in her hour of need. And because he loved her he trusted her. He spoke with his magnificent gesture and told England to be great – showed her quite clearly with argument and fact how an empire could be won; and then made his appeal: in past years you've paid foreigners – Hessians and Swiss and Dutch – to fight your battles. Send them away; come yourselves and fight. Englishmen over the seas want to see *you*.

In December 1915, with the assistance of his brother-in-law, Ralph Brooke, who was an instructor at Woolwich and was willing to testify to George's skills at trigonometry and mathematics, he was commissioned as a second lieutenant in the Royal Garrison Artillery. After

a brief visit to Wales after Christmas, he began a training course at
Weymouth in January 1916.

The Mallorys decided to let The Holt for the duration of the war,
and Ruth and Clare took up residence at Westbrook until George
was able to find some accommodation at Weymouth. Eventually
he found a suitable place at Abbotsbury, a village five miles along
the coast. They soon developed a regular routine. George spent
his weekdays training at Weymouth and then was free to go to
Abbotsbury for the weekend, while Ruth came into Weymouth
twice a week to have lunch with him. George soon found that
military training involved an endless amount of standing around,
which he found hard to tolerate. As he said to Mary Anne O'Malley:
'I begin to perceive that the idea of military education is training
in patience under enforced inertia.' He told her that after a month's
further training at Lydd, he would probably go over to France at
about the end of April:

> I feel so mixed when I think of it – not wanting perfect safety for my own
> sake because I prefer adventure and want anyway to share those risks with
> my friends; but thinking so very differently where Ruth comes in.

George crossed over to France on the night of 4 May 1916. He
spent a week at No.1 Base Depot near Le Havre in final preparation
for active service, learning how to put on a gas mask and to use a
revolver. This drew from him the comment: 'If I saw a German 20 yards
off and he gave me plenty of time to aim, I might hit him.' Finally he
was assigned to the 40th Siege Battery north of Armentières, in the
northern sector of the western front. Although naturally apprehensive,
he expressed to Ruth the sense of satisfaction he felt at being at last
involved in the action:

> To feel that one is 'in for it' at last! Things get stirred up and raked over. The
> irreconcilable wrongness (in a general sense) of war has come very strongly
> upon me. When I have looked upon the good green and blossom of spring
> in this beautiful country and seen beautiful buildings, war has seemed more
> than ever inconceivable and monstrous...

And then, my dear, I have actually turned over and weighed (I suppose this happens to everyone) my own personal courage. Curious how I have found myself going back for reassurance to old football days at Winchester! I have found myself repeating words from one of the little red volumes of Artillery Training – 'such a complete absence of self-interest that he will do his duty in the hour of danger *coolly and accurately*.'

George took an immediate liking to his fellow officers, particularly Lieutenant Bell, with whom he shared a cottage and the command of No.4 gun detachment. He told Ruth:

As I see nothing, practically speaking, of anyone else, it's very lucky I like this man – and that I do. [...] He doesn't shout or swear or drill the men, but they know very well what they have to do and do it keenly; they would be gently and firmly admonished if they didn't. One doesn't often meet real competence so well combined with real Christianity.

He also described his first experience of being under fire:

I've spent some time in an observation post. Plenty of 'em round here: merely high places in the town. We use others nearer the enemy, too. Nothing to be seen of Fritz, but one knows where he is on the map and in a good light could see his trenches. I played the game, on my way to the O.P., of shell-dodging for the first time. Quite an amusing game, given as much protection as we have here – you hear them coming and get out of the way. Under these circumstances, one would be very unlucky to be hit. Stones falling in a gully might be much more dangerous.

It was only some weeks later, however, that he confessed to her that on his first night at the observation post a bullet passed between him and the man walking in front, and added: 'But we settled long ago that there's no reckoning with Death'.

At the end of May the battery moved south to a new position in Picardy. Two days later the bombardment preliminary to the Somme offensive began. George spent much time in the front line sorting out problems in communications. Amidst all the horrors of war his thoughts often returned to the mountains, as he told Arthur Benson:

> It is curious how often I am taken back to the Alps – partly through an association in the code of conduct, and partly I think because of their wonderful cleanness. We're now living in old trenches, indescribably filthy. [...] I had a shocking experience some days ago – two of my signallers killed outright; they were walking a little way behind me carrying a reel of wire and were caught by shrapnel before they had time to dodge into the communication trench; such good fellows too. I've had three other casualties in a short time from my small parties.

And a month later he wrote:

> It's not true in my case that one doesn't mind the horrors of war. But in self-defence they must not be allowed to affect the nerves; I have ceased to have any feelings about corpses unless they disgust my nose; on the other hand it always pains me to see a wounded man. The horrors are no longer horrible but tragedy remains pitiable. I still regret my two signallers; it was a tragic end to hours of good fellowship.

After a few days in mid-August when he was in sole charge of the battery, George spent ten days at a rest camp near Amiens. He described to Ruth the bliss of his first day:

> I lay idly in a lovely field and after tea walked into one of two convenient valleys. It was a perfect day. There was corn standing and corn in sheaves all over the rolling country, and a valley full of trees. The colours were deliciously fresh in the pleasant breeze. You may imagine how I sought the stream which I knew must be winding somewhere among the green glades, how suddenly I came upon it [...] and all the rest.

During George's time at the front he and Ruth exchanged letters virtually on a daily basis. In her letters Ruth wrote describing the routine in life at Godalming, news of her family and especially infor- mation on the progress of baby Clare, and she regularly dispatched parcels of food and other necessaries. In his replies George showed understanding for the problems that Ruth was facing at home and described his thoughts and feelings at being confronted with the realities of war, although he sought to spare her the worst of the details. He soon became inured to the drudgery of trench warfare and found that his mountaineering experience helped him when encountering the worst of the privations.

He was also careful to maintain his intellectual interests. He read as widely as he could and took every opportunity to meet friends and fellow-officers. He was delighted to come across two former Charterhouse boys, who had been in his sixth form, and also a young Winchester master, Maurice Platnauer, later to become a Classics don at Brasenose College, Oxford (where the present writer was one of his pupils), and subsequently to be the Principal of the college. On 20 November he told Ruth:

> Last night I was much cheered by the appearance of Platnauer; Yeo, his brigade doctor; and Falconer, the doctor who is with Chamier. [...] I found myself quite gay, talking about books and art to some extent; and yet I had been so depressed before, that when I heard they were coming I was annoyed. [...] I suppose in common parlance I'm 'wanting leave'.

Leave came through in time for him to spend Christmas 1916 at Westbrook with Ruth and Clare. They had ten days together before George returned to France on Boxing Day. After some weeks at brigade headquarters as assistant to a colonel, George had a short spell as liaison officer with the French artilery before rejoining 40th Siege Battery in time for the British advance in March, when the Germans withdrew from the Somme to the Hindenburg Line.

But now George began to suffer increasing pain from the ankle injury he had sustained at Birkenhead in 1909. It affected him so badly that he found it difficult to walk about in boots. He was examined by a medical officer who concluded that the original injury had been a fracture which had failed to heal properly. He was sent back to England and underwent an operation in London at the beginning of May. On his discharge from hospital he went to Westbrook to convalesce. His recovery was swift and

by the beginning of August he was fit enough to test his ankle in the
mountains. He travelled to Scotland and went over to the Isle of Arran
where he spent several days with David Pye. It was the first time he had
walked on Scottish hills and he found it a pleasant experience:

> The mountains themselves are so lovely, and when one gets up high [...]
> the view of all the islands and peninsulas in those parts is like being in some
> enchanting country – nothing I have seen beats it for colour.

His ankle still gave him some concern, as he reported to his sister
Avie:

> It just managed to do all that was required of it, but with many signs of
> weakness: it used to be very stiff in the evenings and had to be rubbed
> vigorously before use.

But his condition continued to improve and in September the army
doctors passed him fit for duty.

He was posted to Avington Park, an army camp near Winchester,
where he started training on the new sixty-pound guns which had
been acquired by the Royal Artillery. At first he found the quiet of the
camp very strange. He was also frustrated at some of the jobs he was
given. These including watching over the horses and sorting out piles
of discarded socks to make up suitable pairs. But there were compensa-
tions. He was able to visit Winchester where he met Graham Irving.
He also went on some of his favourite walks. One day he completed
22 miles, from Itchen Abbas up the river to Swarraton and Brown
Candover, and back by Old Alresford, Tichborne and Cheriton, an
expedition which he described as 'not bad for a crock like me'. He
also borrowed a motorcycle from one of the masters at Winchester
and made regular weekend visits to Westbrook, which was only about
30 miles from the camp. Ruth was delighted to see him, especially as
she was now expecting their second child.

Their second daughter, Beridge Ruth, was born on 16 September
1917. Geoffrey Young had agreed to act as her godfather, but on the
very day that Beridge was born George and Ruth heard sad news

about Geoffrey. He had been severely wounded in Italy, at the battle of San Gabriele, and his left leg had been amputated above the knee. George hastened to write to Geoffrey's mother:

> I can't tell you how much worse I feel it that he should lose a limb than anyone else I know. [...] I can hardly get to thinking of what the loss will mean to his life: the rush of memories is too strong. We had promised each other days on the mountains together.
>
> I must say one other thing. [...] I never believed in Geoffrey so much as now. He'll be fine in his misfortune – finer than ever; there'll be a gesture to rise above it, still gracefully. He'll be more distinguished too – not by the fact itself but by his beautiful attitude towards it. The greatness of him will be seen more than ever to be in his spiritual endowment – he'll be wonderful always with that; won't he, alert, imaginative and profoundly interested, be happy too?

As soon as he could find an address, he wrote to Geoffrey himself and received the spirited reply that he was expecting:

> I am frankly diverted with the prospect of seeing how far I can work up to my old standard of motion with the aid of a sham leg and my trusty old right! I couldn't at forty-two have bettered my hill-going. Now I shall have the immense stimulus of a new start, with every little inch of progress a joy instead of a commonplace. I count on my great-hearts, like you, to share in the fun of that game with me.

George wrote back at the beginning of December:

> Your last letter altogether delighted me. It's rare to hear the mutilated crying Courage to the whole and safe and I like to hear that word from you. I see that we shan't have exhausted life's store of delights for an arm or leg less. And you're still for the hills – that's splendid all ways; you'll find many friends still there and certainly there shall be a rope's length between us again if we're both alive at the end.

In October 1917 George was promoted to full lieutenant and began a senior officer's course. But one day, as he was dashing back into camp from Westbrook on his borrowed motorcycle, he crashed into the gatepost and crushed his right foot. He told Ruth that his brake had 'failed to act', and he assured her that, although he would not be able to walk for several days, the doctor had said that there would be no lasting damage. In fact he had to spend a month in hospital and it was another month before he could walk comfortably.

When he was passed fit for general service in December George fully expected to be sent back to France, but instead he was posted to a battery commander's course at Lydd. The commander of the course was his brother-in-law Ralph Brooke. Ruth and the two Mallory children came over to stay with the Brooke family at Littlestone, a small seaside village five miles from Lydd. George was able to play an occasional round of golf with Ralph Brooke and to spend Christmas with Ruth at Westbrook. In January 1918 they both attended the wedding of Robert Graves, at which George acted as best man, and at Easter they were delighted to hear the news of Geoffrey Young's engagement to Eleanor Slingsby.

At the end of July George managed to get away for a short climbing holiday in Skye with Ruth, David Pye and Leslie Shadbolt, a friend of David's. They enjoyed five days of perfect weather. For two days they climbed from Sligachan, during which they put up a new route on the north face of Sgurr a' Mhadaidh. They then moved westwards to Glen Brittle. On the final day George led a first ascent of the western buttress of Sròn na Ciche. This climb took six hours and was later described as 'probably the finest buttress climb in Skye'. It is now known as Mallory's Slab and Groove. On their descent they celebrated their success with a bathe in a burn. David Pye described it as a 'glorious bathe, a bathe beyond words', but said that their attempt to evade the midges by staying under the water was only 'of limited usefulness'.

In the spring of 1918 the Germans had launched their last great offensive and at the end of September Mallory received the order to return to France. He spent the last few weeks of the war with the 515th Siege Battery near Arras. His commanding officer was Major Gwilym Lloyd George, the son of the Prime Minister and a future Home Secretary. The unit was positioned some distance behind the front line and, as there was little scope for activity, George found himself organising a sports day for the men beside the sea. The events included a football match and an obstacle race which required the men to strip off their clothes, run into the sea, roll in the waves and then run back. All the fighting was in the south and the capture of Cambrai ended the battle of the Hindenburg Line and Germany began to sue for peace.

On 11 November, after the armistice had been announced, George spent the evening at the officers' club in Cambrai with his brother Trafford, who had been in the Royal Flying Corps since 1916. Trafford was later to have a distinguished career with the Royal Air Force. In December 1943 he was appointed Air Chief Marshal in command of all the air forces in support of the D-Day landings. Tragically, in November 1944, while accompanied by his wife on a flight from London to take up his appointment as allied air commander, South East Asia Command, his plane disappeared over the Alps. The wrecked aircraft was located in June 1945, and the bodies of all those who died were buried in the tiny village of Le Rivier d'Allemont in the foothills of the Alps.

The day after the Armistice George wrote to Ruth describing their meeting:

> I was delighted to see T. He was in tremendous form, happy and gay and full of life. [...] We celebrated peace in Cambrai last night at the Officers' Club, five of us from here, a very agreeable party. It was a good evening altogether [...] with much hilarity and no drunkeness. The prevalent feeling I make out, and in part my own, is simply the elation that comes after a hard game or race of supreme importance, won after a struggle in which everyone has expended himself to the last ounce.

A few days later he expressed his feelings to his father:

> Life presents itself very much to me as a gift. If I haven't escaped so many chances of death as plenty of others, still it is surprising to find myself a survivor, and it's not a lot I have always wanted. There has been so much to be said for being in the good company of the dead. Anyway, it's good to be alive now, partly because this gigantic struggle has been worth while. We haven't fought for any flag-waving jingoism nor for any remote and material political aim, but simply to have a better world to live in.

SEVEN

CHARTERHOUSE 1919-1921

George returned home in the second week of January 1919 and within two weeks of his arrival he took up his old job at Charterhouse. His teaching now was mostly in English with a little history. He found the boys pleasant and responsive and took up the threads of his job with a new zest. The family were now re-established at their old home. Mary Anne O'Malley, who was a frequent visitor there, later wrote a description of its setting:

> All his friends must have their own memories of The Holt, the house at Godalming which was his home for the first seven years of married life. It stood perched on the edge of a steep combe, full of a tangled growth of scrubby oaks and hazels, in which in spite of the houses all about, nightingales and black-caps nested and sang. From windows and garden, the eye travelled across the tree-tops to the playing-fields of Charterhouse, and beyond, down the valley of the Wey, to the hills behind Farnham; while round to the south-west, the great bulk of Hindhead stood up against the sky.

She also described her impression of the house and its atmosphere:

> Perhaps the most individual place of all was George's study – a long, low room on the first floor, with an abundance of books, an immense table presided over by a coloured stone group by Eric Gill, a cast of the Hypnos,

and one or two arm-chairs of mellow and agreeable shabbiness. The black plumes of some Scotch firs cut the sky at the level of the western window. George loved this room and this window. He was exceptionally sensitive to his surroundings always; beauty and ugliness had a kind of spiritual importance for him, beyond their external significance; and the actual material perfection of this house of theirs really contributed to his peace and strength and capacity. [...]

On Sundays and 'halves' the house swarmed with boys; the work of getting to know them was immensely simplified by having a spacious house of his own to invite them to. And friends and colleagues and neighbours were always being brought in – or, more frequently, coming of their own motion. It was such a good house to drop in to! One of the two was always there, it seemed, and the other just coming; there was generally some other friend whom it was delightful to meet or meet again. There was always a welcome, and a meal, and a sense of freedom and well-being for mind and body in that house, with any amount of good talk – over the fire, or in the loggia, or strolling idly about the garden, perching on the low wall or on the great oak seat.

Mary Anne later recalled an occasion which brought home to her the contentment and peace of mind which George drew from his home:

It was before one of his Everest lectures at Charterhouse. We had tea in the study. Mallory was nervous, clouded, and restless. Presently for some reason, he moved over to the window and his eye was caught by the waving firs against a windy western sky. 'Extraordinarily beautiful, that is', he murmured, with a sort of relief breathing from him. Then he turned round with, 'It is a good house to live in – its always doing something to help you like that.' His restlessness left him, and he was appeased and quiet for the remainder of the evening.

But despite this great harmony in his home life, at a deep level George felt unfulfilled in his role as a schoolmaster. Shortly before his return from France he had written to Ruth:

The only possible jar to our happiness will be my personal ambitions. You
must be patient with me, my dearest one.

He wondered how he might find more time for writing. Through his
experience of teaching he had developed his own ideas on education
and he was critical of many public school values and customs. During
the war he had planned a book to which he gave the title *The Book
of Geoffrey*, in which a father drew up an ideal plan for the education
of his son. And in 1917, after reading Alec Waugh's *The Loom of Youth*
while he was in hospital, he had drafted a series of articles analysing
the deficiencies of public schools and outlining an ideal school of the
future. In one passage he imagined a confrontation between himself
and an accusing father:

'I gave you a boy', he seems to say, 'with the unspoilt beauties of boyish
qualities. He wasn't exquisitely refined, nor was he a paragon of virtue, nor
yet supremely talented. He was a decent little chap, truthful, honest and
persevering. He had a gay roguish way of fun, and his laughter was without
malice or contempt. I hardly ever knew him short of a job. He was a creature
of the open air, with an interest quick to be aroused. Books were not of great
interest to him; but he knew how to consult them for information about
birds or flowers or whatever he was pursuing. In all a pleasant companion full
of young curiosity, a healthy animal, a proper English boy. And to me how
much more than that! For he had an open heart; open to me at least, and to
his mother, so that we could easily know him.

And what has school done for my boy? It is a different tale I have to
tell now. My son is a capable athlete; he can take hard knocks and give
them; he won't funk and he knows it; he has any amount of what he
would call "guts". I'm glad of that. And he has something that might pass
at a pinch for manners – a method of light conversation, an assurance,
an address. But of manners in the finer sense, the manners that "makyth
man", he knows little enough. He may offer a glass of lemonade to a
lady, and at best he may do it gracefully. But you are not to imagine that
he puts others before self; he has never a serious thought about their
feelings or their interests. He has no desire to look below the surface
of men's minds, no delicacy of approach, no more than a scant degree

of modesty. Superficial and self-satisfied, he is disastrously equipped for making the best of life.

I cannot discover that he has acquired from any honest thinking the right to a single opinion: and yet he is more than sufficiently opinionated and easily contemptuous of any opposite view. He is no less mentally a coward than he is physically courageous, and as prejudiced as he is dependent. I find his whole scale of values petty and unenlightened, he judges by little forms and conventions without seeing to the heart of things: he will notice a man's tie and his socks without remarking that he is a liar; he will prefer him for being rich; and he will dub him eccentric if he is particularly in earnest. For literature, music, art, he cares nothing, and for Nature little more. He seems to have no interest beyond cricket and a motor bicycle, and no taste beyond the music hall vulgarities. It would be difficult to find anyone more readily bored.

Nice things to say about one's own son! But I have tried to be just. Put him, you might say, in a responsible post and see how he will acquit himself. It would not perhaps be an ignoble performance: and that's so much to the good. But are you to take the credit? We can most of us rub along without making a mess of things. Like others, I expect he will be able to muddle through – you haven't destroyed that capacity. But his education was to give him so much more. Perhaps I am partly to blame. But from the first I was helpless. When I gave him to you, he was lost to me. I knew him no longer and couldn't know him. [...] His lips indeed spoke but his heart was closed from me and from his mother. We gave you youth with the bloom of childhood – you have rendered, not indeed Man, but youth again with Man's hard skin.'

George had developed his ideas further in a twelve-page letter which he had sent to Geoffrey Young in February 1918 in which he summarised his conclusions on the ideal school of the future. He felt that the separation between 'School' and 'Home' must be broken down: parents must be given more responsibility than merely the arrangement of holiday fun. Ways must be found to enable parents and teachers to work together. The gulf between the world of school and that of work must also be bridged. His ideal school would have a farm to provide experience of useful employment. He considered that it was necessary to reduce the gap between 'work' and 'play', 'lessons' and 'leisure', and to overcome the belief that mental effort was not an enjoyable part of life. He also felt that the stress laid on the importance of organised games should be reduced and that greater encouragement should be given to other outdoor pursuits, and also to crafts.

George invited his friends Geoffrey Young and David Pye over to The Holt to discuss the feasibility of founding a school of their own. George himself prepared a draft prospectus. The underlying principle was that parents should actively co-operate in all the efforts of the school, so that term and holidays should be complementary influences in a continuous process of education. School reports should be of a more general nature, giving brief accounts of any particularly interesting course of lessons and describing any school enterprise involving the communal activity of the pupils, such as farming. Opportunities should be provided for pupils to develop initiative and self-reliance and they should be encouraged to meet those belonging to a different social class to their own. George's criticism of a socially divisive and totally examination-based educational system was years ahead of his time and still has relevance today. But nothing came of the idea of founding a new school, although both David Pye and Geoffrey Young maintained their interest in the world of education. Pye, a distinguished engineer, later became Provost of University College, London, while Young gave active support to Kurt Hahn in the foundation of Gordonstoun.

In his lessons at Charterhouse George tried to promote an understanding of current political affairs and the creation of that better world for which he believed the war had been fought. He was encouraged by the first sessions of the League of Nations, and in one of his lectures he argued for a new form of patriotism:

If the individual man is conscious of himself as belonging to various groups, to the family, the trade, the class, and many others, why should his group consciousness stop with the state? Why should not an Englishman become conscious of Europe as a group and then of the whole world; become, in fact, a citizen of the world?

His eagerness to support the cause of the League of Nations is seen in the letter he wrote in June 1920 to Gilbert Murray, the Regius

Professor of Greek at Oxford. Murray, whose son Basil was in his final
year at Charterhouse, was the secretary of the Union of the League
of Nations, a voluntary group set up to support the League. George
asked Murray whether the Union could find any use for his services
saying: 'It is a cause which I want to serve, and I am prepared to give
up my present job.' After outlining his experience as a lecturer and
a historian, he added: 'Perhaps the most important thing about me
which I ought to tell you is that I think and feel passionately about
international politics.' George was clearly serious in his application, for
he told Murray he was willing to visit him in Oxford that weekend.
He also told Frank Fletcher that if his application was successful he
would leave Charterhouse at the end of the summer term. But in the
event nothing came of this approach.

During the Christmas holidays of 1920 George paid a visit to
Ireland. He wanted to gain deeper understanding of what life was
like in the country as the situation deteriorated in the bitter struggle
between the IRA and the British government, backed by its ruthless
counter-insurgency force, the Black and Tans. To facilitate his visit
George had a useful contact in Conor O'Brien, an Irish climber who
had been a regular member of the Pen y Pass house parties before
the war. O'Brien himself had been a Republican gun-runner and
he introduced George to such leading nationalist figures as Erskine
Childers, the author of the famous spy story, *The Riddle of the Sands*,
and Desmond Fitzgerald. Fitzgerald, who had been in prison with De
Valera, the Sinn Féin president, had the post of 'director of propaganda'
at the Dáil, the assembly of the provisional Irish government, and he
provided George with a pass. On the back of George's photograph
he wrote:

> Mr G. Mallory is anxious to have first-hand information as to acts of
> oppression and terror. I shall be glad if he can be assisted.

During the week he spent in Dublin, George felt his sympathies
gradually being drawn to favour a people who were ready to fight
for their independence. Despite the apparent normality of life, he
was very conscious of the oppressive atmosphere, and he described

Dublin Castle as a 'place not only of blood and iron, of machine guns and barbed wire, and of bolts and bars, but also of secret and sinister chambers where strange things happen in darkness'. He was taken on a trip into rural areas where he heard of summary executions performed by the Black and Tans, and he met the families of Republicans who had died fighting the British forces. Although he behaved cautiously and tried to avoid contact with the counter-insurgency forces, he had one disturbing experience. One night he was woken in his lodgings at 1.30 a.m. and questioned by a visitor with a flashlight in one hand and a revolver in the other:

> He asked me finally, was I a Protestant? I told him my father was a clergyman in the Church of England. And that settled it. My room was not searched. I blessed my English accent and lay awake for a long while cogitating that irrelevant and impertinent question. Was I a Protestant? Was he living in Dublin? And hadn't he discovered yet that Protestants and Roman Catholics are equally Sinn Féiners?
>
> I was glad in any case that no search was made, for my landlady's sake and perhaps for my own too. I knew what a search might mean. I had been taken shortly after I came to Dublin to see a young lady's flat. The party who had visited it the night before had done their work thoroughly. What I saw was an illustration of chaos.

Mallory was very upset by what he heard and saw and, although he did not condone the violence of the Irish, he gradually came to an understanding of the ideal for which they were striving:

> There has been wrong on both sides: but national inspirations, a passionate idealism, are to be found only on one side. It is to this fact that Irishmen appeal when they exclaim, 'If only people in England knew! If only they would come and see!' They believe in the truth of their idealism. But how are they to project a message from this spirit to penetrate English apathy? They say to Englishmen 'Come and see.' They believe that for Englishmen in general to see would be enough. And it is enough!

In 1919 the mountain gatherings at Pen y Pass had started again. Geoffrey Young had written to George from Florence:

> I am keen to revive all the hill activities at once and count on you, as almost the only survivor, to do the work of bringing in the young folk. We will do the social side, if you will set the climbing standard.

Young calculated that out of sixty climbers whose names were recorded in the Pen y Pass book, twenty-three had died in the war and eleven had been injured. One of the most remarkable survivors was Rawson Owen, the proprietor of the Gorphwysfa Hotel. Despite the fact that he had been badly wounded in the Boer War, he had signed up in 1914 and, after taking part in the Gallipoli campaign, had fought in Palestine before ending up in France 'sound and unwounded, one of the few original survivors of his regiment'. Young himself was determined to try to climb again, and he designed a special artificial limb with a detachable leg and a variety of soles, including a steel spike studded with nails.

That Easter, a party of twenty-eight, exceeding all Young's expectations, gathered in Wales to enjoy perfect weather in the mountains. George bought a second-hand car for the occasion, a 1912 American Studebaker-Flanders four-cylinder, five-seater tourer. The most remarkable achievement was that of Geoffrey Young, who on Easter Day, watched and encouraged by many of his friends, made his first one-legged climb, ascending the Milestone Ridge and the Gashed Crag to gain the summit of Tryfan. For climbs on Lliwedd, George assisted him by driving his car along the track to Llyn Llydaw and then backing into the lake to turn. Geoffrey summed up his renewed hopes in a memorable poem:

> I have not lost the magic of long days:
> I live them, dream them still.
> Still am I master of the starry ways,
> and freeman of the hill.
> Shattered my glass, ere half the sands had run –
> I hold the heights, I hold the heights I won.

On Easter Monday George, in company with Ruth, David Pye and Claude Elliott, invented a new traverse of the East buttress of Lliwedd, which was given the name Garter Traverse, because it lay 200ft below the well-known Girdle Traverse. The climb was repeated later by Harold Porter, who wrote:

This climb is peculiarly typical of Mallory, and bears witness, perhaps more than any other of his discoveries in Britain, to his fertility in invention and his resourcefulness in action. the standard almost throughout is severe; and the first pitch, which is of unique character, is exceptionally severe.

In July, George returned to the Alps with Claude Elliott and Harold Porter. Later, at a meeting of the Alpine Club, he described his feelings at his first sight of the mountains:

I had not seen them now for seven years. Still, I had thought about them not a little; I had diligently read the *Alpine Journal*; I had reminded myself of their features by studying photographs. And yet their appearance as we were coming up towards St Gervais was beyond belief, an appearance quite unconnected with any recollections, a startlingly fresh new vision, new as when I first saw the Alps, new so that I seemed never to have seen them before.

As they were ascending in the electric train from St Gervais, George found himself discussing the mountain scene with a young Frenchman who seemed very knowledgeable.

He was able to name every point which I had forgotten or never knew, and seemed to know of every ascent on this side, to the last gendarme, from the Charmoz to the Midi. I had little doubt that he had an ambitious programme and though I had no intention of referring to my own performances, I began to question him about his. He made no difficulty about telling me. He climbed with two other Frenchmen, always without guides; and the story of his conquests came tremulously forth, his eyes shining with enthusiasm. It was not a long story; and it was a modest record, incredibly modest. I was amazed that so much mountain-lore as he evidently possessed should be expended on so little. 'Je ne suis pas fort,' he said simply in explanation. But the party, he confided, if they could get really fit, intended as a crowning exploit to ascend Mont Blanc this year from the Grands Mulets.

I have said that I intended not to speak about my own achievements or projects. [...] However it seemed necessary to break my resolution; and I mentioned that I had twice been to the top of Mont Blanc. The Frenchman [...] questioned me eagerly and insisted upon hearing everything. I felt that I never had met so passionate a mountain-lover.

George's party had a slightly disappointing start to their season: they had to turn back below the summit of the Requin because they were unfit and were running out of time. Two days later they went up to the Col du Géant and the Rifugio Torino. On their arrival at the hut they met a party of Italians. Porter recorded in his diary:

A party of seven exuberant Italians hailed us cheerfully on arrival and an amusing dialogue in French was held between them and George.

The Italians: 'Hurrah for the brave Americanoes! It was you and we who won the war.' George (pretending to be pleased): 'Ah, you do us too much honour. The credit all belongs to you gallant Frenchmen!'

The next day they were unable to do a big climb because Elliott's knee let him down and he had to return to England. Mallory and Porter then decided to climb the Aiguille des Grands Charmoz from the Glacier de Trélaport: this had been climbed only once before, in 1899. The climbing proved to be extremely severe, and George wrote a full account of their ascent in a paper delivered to the Alpine Club in the following year. As he told David Pye: 'For sustained endeavour and dramatic moments the climb far exceeded any rock climb I know.' Their last major climb that year was the traverse of Mont Blanc from the Quintino Sella hut, descending to the Grands Mulets.

After his return to England George summed up his impressions of the 1919 season in a letter to Geoffrey Young:

We were only out a fortnight [...] but it was a wonderful time. It was thrilling, beyond anything I can keep in my head to imagine, merely to see the snow peaks again. And then I was so fit myself. I had so many doubts how I should feel, particularly about snow and ice, after seven years; and my dear Geoffrey, I can say it to you, I was so much better than I had reason to expect.

After joining Ruth and the children for a few days at the seaside, in September George took Ruth on a walking holiday near Gloucester. He later told David Pye:

R and I had a wonderful week in the West Country, walking many miles in the fairest land of all. The Wye, the Monnow west of Monmouth, the Teme, and the Severn were our beat. R went splendidly and walked thirty-one and twenty-four miles on two consecutive days. We just walked steadily on, lingering occasionally for a meal in a country inn or on a grassy bank commanding the view, or to eat red apples in an orchard, enjoying all the detail and the distance till some golden beauty seemed to have been distilled all about us.

In 1920 Geoffrey Young became president of the Climbers' Club. Realising that the club was now in serious need of reinvigoration, he asked George to edit the next issue of the *Climbers' Club Journal*. George spent much of the summer of 1920 collecting material for this edition. His friends rallied round with contributions and in November he produced what Geoffrey Young described as 'the best number of any journal'. George himself wrote a review of *Mountain Craft*, a book edited by Geoffrey Young, which had been published in October. He had enjoyed discussing its philosophy on long evenings in the smoking room at Pen y Pass before the war, and he now described it as 'the most important work on mountaineering which has appeared in this generation'.

At Easter that year there was the usual gathering at Pen y Pass and towards the end of July George left for what was to prove his last Alpine season. His companions were Herbert Read, David Pye and Claude Elliott. In the event this was a disappointing time. Several expeditions had to be called off because of bad weather. Their most successful outings were the traverse of the Matterhorn from Courmeyer and the ascent of the Rothorn from the Triftjoch. George arrived home on the morning of 21 August to find that a son, John, had been born just half an hour earlier. A few days later he reported to Geoffrey:

> Ruth's baby was born last Saturday – a thumping great bruiser of a boy with fists and feet, a chin and very fat cheeks as salient features. We're highly delighted and Ruth is as bright and well as possible. He arrived ten days early and created some consternation. Ruth had to be conveyed here from Westbrook in a neighbour's motor car at an early hour in the morning; the monthly nurse arrived only an hour before the birth and I reached home from the Alps only half an hour after it.

During the winter of 1920 George became increasingly restless. He had now come to the firm conviction that he needed a change of career from teaching. He wanted a job which would stretch his abilities further and would provide an opportunity to do some writing. He had in fact already decided to leave Charterhouse at the end of the summer term, when in January 1921 he received a letter from Captain Percy Farrar, a former president of the Alpine Club, asking whether he was interested in joining an expedition to Mount Everest. For two years there had been growing talk of the possibility of sending an expedition to climb the highest mountain in the world. Nepal remained closed to travellers, but in December 1920 permission had been granted to enter Tibet, and it seemed that an attempt on Everest would now go forward.

EIGHT

EVEREST: THE ULTIMATE CHALLENGE

In 1920 the ascent of Everest symbolised the supreme challenge to human endeavour remaining on earth. Two of mankind's greatest aspirations had recently been achieved. The American explorer Robert Peary had been the first to reach the North Pole in April 1909. Two years later, in December 1911, the Norwegian Roald Amundsen had narrowly beaten Captain Scott in a dash to the South Pole. Everest's status as the world's highest mountain had only been recognised some seventy years earlier. It stands on the borders of Nepal and Tibet, countries which then were both closed to Europeans. When viewed from India, Everest does not stand out as a pre-eminent mountain. Many of the surrounding peaks appear to be higher. Until 1846 Nanda Devi, 25,479ft high and originally labelled A2, was thought to be the world's highest peak. Then for a brief period that accolade was awarded to Kanchenjunga at 28,176 feet. Everest's pre-eminence was only established in 1852 through the work of the Great Trigonometrical Survey of India.

The Great Himalayan Range, which contains the highest peaks on earth, forms a barrier, 1,500 miles long and seldom falling below 18,000ft in height, across the northern frontier of India. More than ninety of its summits are known to exceed 24,000ft. This mighty mountain chain was regarded with awe and reverence by those who dwelt in the foothills south of the range. They considered this area to be the dwelling-place of the gods and they built monasteries in remote places high up on the flanks of the mountains. They also barred access through the valleys and over the high passes to all foreigners.

When the British took over responsibility for the rule of India at the beginning of the nineteenth century, one of their first acts was to institute the Great Trigonometrical Survey of India, with the intention of mapping the whole area. The originator of the survey and its first superintendent was Colonel William Lambton. On his death in January 1823 he was succeeded by his assistant, George Everest (whose name was actually pronounced 'Eve-rest'), who completed the main survey in 1841. He returned to England two years later and in 1861 was honoured with a knighthood.

As the surveyors neared completion of the main survey they began to take an increasing interest in the position and height of the great snow peaks over 100 miles away to the north in Nepal. British surveyors were banned from Nepal and so the problems confronting the survey were immense. They had the task of mapping some 20,000 square miles of remote and wild territory, from which they themselves were excluded. In his book *The Great Arc*, John Keay dramatically describes their efforts:

> Pelted by hailstones, their tents ablaze from the lightning and their trail obliterated by blizzards, the men of the Survey would dig in and wait. Survival depended on merino drawers, Harris tweeds and alpaca overcoats. Their boots were leather, and they ate mostly rice. They might be marooned for weeks. Then, without warning, in the chill first light of day when the cloud had unaccountably overslept in the valleys, their patience would at last be rewarded. Sailing a sea of cumulus beneath an azure sky, a line of glistening summits would loom remotely from the ether.

From their position on the northern Indian plain the surveyors took observations as opportunity offered towards the high Himalayan peaks. Gradually fixed points and altitudes began to appear on the survey sheets. For working purposes each summit was given a Roman numeral. One mountain was labelled Peak XV. In 1850, after taking observations from six different stations, James Nicholson, one of the assistant surveyors, became convinced that this mountain was the highest in the area, but it was not until two years later that the result of his observations were finally calculated. There is a story, no doubt apocryphal, that in 1852 Alexander Waugh, who had suceeded George Everest as Surveyor-General, was sitting in the offices of the Survey of India at Dehra Dun when an excited official burst into his room and announced that he had 'discovered the world's highest mountain'. Waugh wanted to be completely sure that Peak XV was the highest mountain in the world before making an official announcement and he spent four years checking the calculations. At last in March 1856, he wrote to his deputy, Captain Thuiller, who was based in Calcutta, directing his attention to Peak XV and continued:

> We have for some years known that this mountain is higher than any hitherto measured in India and most probably it is the highest in the whole world. I was taught by my respected chief and predecessor Colonel Sir Geo. Everest to assign to every geographical object its true local or native appellation. [...] But here is a mountain, most probably the highest in the world, without a local name that we can discover. [...] In the meantime the privilege as well as the duty devolves on me to assign to this lofty pinnacle of our globe a name whereby it may be known among geographers and become a household word among civilized nations.
>
> In virtue of this privilege, in testimony to my affectionate respect for my revered chief, in conformity with what I believe to be the wish of all the members of the scientific department over which I have the honour to preside, and to perpetuate the memory of that illustrious master of accurate geographical research, I have determined to name this noble peak of the Himalayas Mont [sic] Everest.

He calculated the height above sea level to be 29,002ft. This figure has subsequently been adjusted on several occasions. The most recent estimate, based on global positional satellites, gives Everest's height as 29,035ft.

Waugh's name for the mountain was endorsed by the Secretary of State for India and by the Royal Geographical Society. For a few years doubts remained whether Everest was in fact the highest mountain in the world. A survey of the Karakoram mountains to the far north-west was still in process from Kashmir. This range, and one peak in particular to which the label K2 was given, clearly reached a very great height. But in 1858 the Kashmir survey revealed that K2 at 28,287ft, although higher than Kanchenjunga, yielded in supremacy to Mount Everest.

Although Everest's supreme height was swiftly conceded, dispute continued over the name which Waugh had given to the peak. Brian Hodgson, a distinguished Buddhist scholar who had lived in Kathmandu for some years, proposed that the mountain should be given the Nepali name Devadhanga. A committee, convened by Waugh to consider the matter, swiftly concluded that Devadhanga was 'indefinite and unacceptable'. Apparently the name applied to the group of peaks in the area and so would not be appropriate for the world's highest mountian. In the event, the argument over Everest's name was rendered irrelevant by the outbreak of the Indian Mutiny in May 1857, just over a year after Waugh's pronouncement. By the time the mutiny had been suppressed, the name Mount Everest had won recognition throughout the world.

The problem in finding a native name for Everest lay in its inaccessible position. As Sir Francis Younghusband explained in his introduction to *Mount Everest, The Reconnaissance 1921*:

Mount Everest for its size is a singularly shy and retiring mountain. It hides itself away behind other mountains. On the north side, in Tibet, it does indeed stand up proudly and alone, a true monarch among mountains. But it stands in a very sparsely inhabited part of Tibet, and very few people ever go to Tibet. From the Indian side only its tip appears among a mighty array of peaks which being nearer look higher. Consequently for a long time no one suspected Mount Everest of being the supreme mountain not only of the Himalaya but of the world. [...] No native name for it could be discovered. [...] From the Tibetan side it is much more conspicuous and [...] as Colonel Howard-Bury found in 1921 the Tibetans call it Chomolungmo, which Colonel Howard-Bury translated, the 'Goddess Mother of the Mountains' – a most appropriate name. But the name Mount Everest is now so firmly established throughout the world that it would be impossible to change it.

Before 1800 very few explorers had made their way through the Himalayan valleys or crossed the high passes into Nepal. Most of these early travellers were Jesuit missionaries. After the control of India passed to the British, further knowledge came from military expeditions into the area. Occasionally an officer brought back a hastily made map of the route, or a sketch of the peaks which had been seen from some high pass. After the recognition of Everest's pre-eminence, further efforts were made to achieve a more accurate survey of the area. Since there was no question of Europeans being allowed into Tibet, in 1860 Captain Montgomerie of the Indian Survey took the decision to train Indians in the use of survey instruments, so that they could measure the altitude and position of the high peaks. These Indian surveyors, know as the Pundit Explorers, made hazardous journeys into the moumtains, knowing that they would face torture and death if it was discovered that they were working for the British. They were away for months, and sometimes years at a time. Their explorations were so secret that not even their names were revealed and they were referred to by two letters. Two of the most famous who explored the Everest region were Kalian Singh, known as 'AK' and Hari Ram, 'MH'. Captain John Noel, who himself made a secret journey through Tibet in 1913, described how they operated:

> They counted every step by the revolution of their prayer wheels, or by the beads of their rosaries. At night they would write their notes on a roll of paper hidden inside the prayer wheel. They recorded compass bearings of mountains and rivers passed, by means of little compasses cleverly disguised as amulets worn round their necks. They carried boiling point thermometers inside hollow walking sticks for the measurement of altitudes. Some pretended to be pilgrims and others traders, carrying medicines in order to ingratiate themselves with the lamas and officers they met in Tibet.

The information which they brought back by these means was surprisingly accurate and proved invaluable to the surveyors of the Himalayan region.

In 1856, at the time when Everest's supremacy was first recognised, mountaineering was in its infancy. Mont Blanc had first been climbed in 1786 but it was the ascent of the Wetterhorn in 1854 by

Alfred Wills that had led to the development of mountaineering as a sporting pastime. The foundation of the Alpine Club in 1857 insti-gated the rapid exploration of the Alps as successive peaks were scaled, including the tragic ascent of the Matterhorn by Edward Whymper in 1865. Snow and ice techniques showly improved and the thoughts of mountaineers turned to wider horizons. In 1892 Martin Conway led an expedition to the Karakoram range in the Himalayas, taking with him four members of the Gurkha tribe as porters on the mountain. His expedition was financed by the Royal Society and the Royal Geographical Society and represented the first full-scale effort at climbing a Himalayan mountain.

The question was now being raised whether Everest could be climbed, and, if so, how might one approach the mountain. Probably the first person to propose that an attempt should be made was a young captain in the 5th Gurkha Regiment of the Indian Army, Charles Granville Bruce. In 1893 he suggested the idea to the explorer and diplomat, Francis Younghusband, who at that time was the political agent in Chitral on the North-West Frontier. Younghusband himself was an adventurous and experienced traveller. In 1886 he had explored Manchuria, and in the following year he had made an astonishing journey across the Gobi Desert and the Karakoram mountains from Peking to Rawalpindi. Because of the political situation, however, plans for climbing Mount Everest were taken no further, although Bruce made several expeditions into the Himalayas, accompanied by selected Gurkhas from his regiment.

In 1903, following a Tibetan attack on Sikkim, Francis Younghusband was sent with a military escort to Lhasa, the Tibetan caspital. His instruc-tions were to secure the withdrawal of the Tibetans from Sikkim, a state allied by treaty with British India, and then to establish trade relations with Tibet. Younghusband successfully achieved this difficult and dangerous mission and was rewarded by a knighthood on his return. While he was in Tibet he sent two officers into the west of the country to view the approaches to Everest. From a distance of 60 miles they scanned the north face of the mountain and thought that it might be possible to climb the north ridge. Another of his officers managed to take a photograph of Everest from the town of Kampa Dzong, over 90 miles away. Younghusband himself went to Kampa Dzong and later described how from his tent he saw dawn breaking over Everest, 'poised high in heaven as the spotless pinnacle of the world'.

In 1907 it was proposed that the fiftieth anniversary of the Alpine Club should be marked by making a reconnaissance of Mount Everest. This suggestion was supported by Charles Bruce, now promoted to general. In view of political changes in the area, such an expedition seemed a more feasible prospect. The treaty which Younghusband had secured with Tibet had marked a definite softening of the attitude of the Dalai Lama and his advisers towards the admission of foreigners into Tibet. But when an expedition was formally proposed, the Secretary of State for India refused to give permission because of what he termed 'considerations of high Imperial policy'. Since Nepal remained closed to all Europeans except for the political representative of the British Indian government, an official expedition to Everest seemed out of the question.

The urge to make the attempt, however, remained as strong as ever. In 1913 John Noel, a young lieutenant of the East Yorkshire Regiment, who had travelled extensively on the India–Tibet border, decided to try to examine Everest from close quarters. Accompanied by a small party of hill tribesmen, he set out from Darjeeling, disguised as an Indian Muslim. After several weeks of travel through unmapped country they found a high pass which was not under the surveillance of border guards and slipped into southern Tibet. They then continued westward towards the northern approach to Everest. As he was crossing another pass, Noel had a clear view of a chain of snowy peaks ahead of him. Suddenly, as the clouds shifted, he saw far away over the crests of nearer mountains, 'a glittering spire of rock fluted with snow'. From its magnetic bearing he realised that this could only be Everest, which he estimated to be about 60 miles away.

After continuing his journey Noel encountered some Nepalese traders who told him that there was a monastery high up a neighbouring valley, from which a close view of a huge mountain which they called Kangchen Lemboo Geudyong might be obtained. As he set off up this valley Noel was pursued by Tibetan guards and, when they became hostile, he fired a shot above their heads. The guards rode away in retreat but Noel's companions refused to go any further and, much to his disappointment, he had no alternative but to turn back. As he later commented:

> Within forty miles and nearer at that time than any white man had been! I leave you to imagine my chagrin and disappointment.

A year later Noel was invited to join a group of climbers and surveyors who were planning a two-stage attempt on Everest. There was to be a reconnaissance in 1915 to be followed by a full-scale attempt in the following year. These plans were supported by the Royal Geographical Society and the Alpine Club. The expedition was to be led by Cecil Rawling, a soldier who had taken part in the frontier campaigns of 1897–98. He had later worked as a surveyor on the Tibetan border and in 1903 had mapped over 40,000 square miles of Himalayan territory. John Buchan, a close friend of his, offered to help with the planning of the expedition. Rawling had no illusions about the magnitude of his task and wrote:

> It may well be that Mount Everest is unclimbable on the north side by any mountaineer, however skilled, or that even if the mountaineering difficulties were not insuperable, the altitude makes human advance impossible. These questions however have not yet been settled, and it is the aim of the expedition to do something towards their solution.

Unfortunately the outbreak of war in August that year prevented any further progress, and Cecil Rawling was killed at Ypres two months later. In his obituary in *The Times*, John Buchan noted how 'the outbreak of war put a stop to those pleasant fancies'.

The slaughter of the First World War took its toll of a generation of climbers. In addition to those like Cecil Rawling and Siegfried Herford who were killed, many were severely wounded. Geoffrey Winthrop Young, who was regarded as Britain's finest alpine mountaineer, lost a leg, and Charles Bruce was severly wounded in the Gallipoli campaign, but the question of Everest refused to go away. In March 1919 the Royal Geographical Society invited John Noel to give a lecture to its members describing his secret journey to Tibet in 1913. When later that year Sir Francis Younghusband became president of the Society, in a stirring address he eagerly promoted an expedition to climb Mount Everest:

> The accomplishment of such a feat will elevate the human spirit and will give man, especially us geographers, a feeling that we really are getting the upper hand on the earth, and that we are acquiring a true mastery of our surroundings. As long as we impotently creep about at the foot of these mighty mountains and gaze at their summits without attempting to ascend them, we entertain towards them a too excessive feeling of awe. [...]
>
> If man stands on earth's highest summit, he will have an increased pride in himself in the struggle for ascendancy over matter. This is the incalculable good which the ascent of Mount Everest will confer.

In April 1920 a joint meeting was held with the Alpine Club to determine the objectives of such an expedition. Although there was some disagreement between the aims of the geographers, of mapping and surveying the area, and those of the mountaineers, of climbing to the summit, agreement was reached that the principal object of the expedition should be the ascent of the mountain, and that all preliminary reconnaissance should be directed towards that aim. The Royal Geographical Society would undertake the organisation up to the establishment of a base camp, and the Alpine Club would be responsible for the climbing arrangements on the mountain.

Although political difficulties still remained, there was some ground for optimism in the fact that in 1919 Lord Curzon had become the Secretary of State for Foreign Affairs. In his earlier days as Viceroy of India, he had strongly supported an attempt on Everest. At this juncture Lieutenant-Colonel Charles Howard-Bury, who came from a wealthy and well-connected family and was an experienced Himalayan traveller, offered to go to India and Tibet at his own expense and try to secure permission for an expedition. For the next six months he conducted complicated negotiations between the Viceroy, the Governor of Bengal, the Commander-in-Chief of British forces in India, and the political officer in Sikkim. He had meetings with the

Surveyor-General of the Indian Survey and also held discussions with the Tibetan authorities. Finally, Sir Charles Bell, the political officer in Sikkim, who had established good relations with the Dalai Lama, was instructed to go to Tibet to ask permission for a climbing expedition to Mount Everest. At an audience with the Dalai Lama on 9 December 1920, Bell was given the approval of the Tibetan government for such a venture. The final hurdle had been overcome and plans for a Mount Everest expedition were now set in motion.

NINE

PLANS FOR A RECONNAISSANCE 1921

In January 1921 the Royal Geographical Society and the Alpine Club jointly established a Mount Everest Committee, with Sir Francis Younghusband as chairman. Since there was potential for disagreement between the aims of the geographers and those of the climbers, it was agreed that the expedition should be undertaken in two stages. In the first year the main aim would be to survey the area around Everest in order to produce an accurate map of the mountain and its approaches, while in the second year a serious attempt would be made to reach the summit. To prevent any misunderstanding a formal resolution was passed to this effect:

> The main object this year is reconnaissance. This does not debar the moun-
> tain party from climbing as high as possible on a favourable route, but
> attempts on a particular route must not be prolonged to hinder the comple-
> tion of the reconnaissance.

The climbing party was to consist of four members, chosen by the Alpine Club. The first to be approached was George Mallory. On 22 January Captain Percy Farrar, one of the three Alpine Club members on the Everest Committee and a former president of the club, wrote to George asking whether he was interested in going on the expedition:

It looks as though Everest would really be tried this summer. Party would
leave early April and get back in October. Any aspirations?

Although George was pleased to be invited, he knew that membership
of the expedition would involve a long separation from his young
family, and he was uncertain at first whether he should accept. For
some time he had been trying to formulate plans for his future if he
gave up his teaching post at Charterhouse and, as he confided to David
Pye, he was now 'faced with a problem which throws all others into
the background – Everest'.

He was still unsure what to do and was feeling inclined to refuse
the invitation, when Geoffrey Young came down to visit him in
Godalming. Geoffrey quickly persuaded George and Ruth that this
would be an extraordinary adventure. It was an opportunity not to
be missed and would have an important bearing on George's future
career. Ruth was won over by Geoffrey's arguments and agreed that
George should go. George himself quickly came to realise what a great
opportunity he was being given. As he wrote to his sister Avie:

> I hope it won't appear to you a merely fantastic performance. I was inclined
> to regard it as such when the idea was first mooted a few weeks ago, but
> it has come to appear now, with the help of Ruth's enthusiasm, rather as
> the opportunity of a lifetime. [...] The future bears an adventurous aspect
> altogether; I have resigned my mastership at Charterhouse, as I intended to
> do in any case after the summer. I shall be starting for Tibet early in April and
> have no very definite idea what I shall do after I come back in the autumn
> – except that there's much in my head which is asking to be written.

On 9 February he was invited to a lunch in Mayfair to meet three
representatives of the Mount Everest Commmittee, including the
chairman. Over lunch Younghusband gave George a formal invitation
to join the expedition, and was surprised to note that he accepted
'without visible emotion' and was not 'bursting with enthusiasm'.
But Younghusband was impressed by his quiet determination as one
who was:

conscious of his own powers and of the position he had won by his own exertions; and he had, in consequence, a not obtrusive but [...] quite justifiable pride in himself as a mountaineer.

He later noted that:

Mallory actually leaving for Everest was a different man from Mallory somewhat passively receiving the invitation. The joy of great struggle was clearly arising.

In a letter to Young, Mallory gave his own account of the meeting:

I lunched with Farrar yesterday to meet Raeburn and Younghusband, and the old boy made me a formal offer which I accepted. It seems rather a momentous step altogether, with a new job to find when I come back, but it will not be a bad thing to give up the settled ease of this present life.

It had always been Younghusband's intention that Charles Bruce should lead the expedition. It was Bruce who had first suggested to him the idea of climbing Everest when they were together in Chitral nearly thirty years earlier. As Younghusband wrote:

General Bruce, who had had the idea in his mind for so many years, who knew the Himalaya as no one else did, and who had a special aptitude for handling Himalayan people, was now in England, and it was to him our thought first turned.

But Bruce had been invalided out of the Army in 1919, after three Army medical boards assessed him as suffering from cardiac debility, and he had been told to take a quiet life. For a man of his disposition this was an impossibility and he had begun to climb again and had also recently taken up a position with the Glamorgan Territorial Association. He did not feel that he could readily ask for leave of absence and it was also felt by the committee that, since the main aim in 1921 was the surveying and mapping of the area, he should be reserved to lead the second expedition, planned for 1922, which would have the primary objective of reaching the summit of the mountain. And so the leadership of the 1921 expedition was given to Charles Howard-Bury. He was a well-connected Old Etonian and former Army officer with a large estate at Mulingar in Ireland. He had travelled extensively in the Himalayas and in the previous year had been largely instrumental in securing the political approval of the Tibetan government for the expedition. His main interest lay in exploration and, although he had a good knowledge of mountains, he was not a mountaineer in the technical sense.

Harold Raeburn, an experienced Scottish mountaineer, was chosen to lead the climbing party. He had a fine record of guideless climbing in the Alps and in 1920 had reached 21,000ft on Kanchenjunga. But it soon became apparent that he was not in the best of health and, at fifty-six, his age was against him. A second climber with Himalayan experience was Dr Alexander Kellas, also a Scotsman. He was a lecturer in chemistry at the Middlesex Hospital in London. He had unrivalled knowledge of Himalayan travel, having spent several months every year exploring the remoter valleys and passes in order to further his study of the physiological effects of climbing at high altitudes. He had also experimented with the use of oxygen and in 1920 had climbed to a height of 23,400ft on Mount Kamet in Garhwal. But, at fifty-three, he also was disadvantaged by his age.

The two younger members of the climbing party were George Mallory and George Finch. Finch, who had been born in Australia but had lived for much of his life in Switzerland, had a considerable reputation as an alpine climber, although he did not fit easily into the social milieu which dominated British climbing at the time. He wore long hair and was forthright and uncompromising in his views. Three years earlier he had divorced his wife, a fact that he sought to conceal from the Everest Committee. During the war he had been awarded the MBE for his service with a bomb disposal unit and in 1921 he was teaching chemistry at Imperial College, London.

Provision was also made for the surveying and mapping activities of the expedition. It was arranged that two officers of the Indian Survey Department, Major Henry Morshead and Major Edward Wheeler, would join the expedition in India. Morshead had considerable experience of travelling on the eastern borders of Tibet. Wheeler, although he was recruited for his surveying abilities, was also a keen climber and a member of the Canadian Alpine Club. Also joining them in India would be Dr A.M. Heron, of the Indian Geological Survey. Dr Alexander Wollaston, who had made extensive journeys in East Africa and in the interior of New Guinea, was appointed medical officer and naturalist to the expedition.

It was estimated that the cost of the two stages of the expedition in 1921 and 1922 would be in the region of £10,000. Appeals for contributions were made to members of the Royal Geographical Society and the Alpine Club. Members of the Alpine Club subscribed over £3,000 and Fellows of the Royal Geographical Society raised a similar sum. With the assistance of John Buchan a deal was concluded with *The Times* for exclusive coverage of the expedition. Arrangements were also made with the *Daily Graphic* for the publication of photographs.

In the weeks before leaving for India George found himself several times in conflict with Arthur Hinks, the Everest Committee secretary. This tension illustrated the uneasy alliance between the Royal Geographical Society, with its aims of surveying and mapping, and the Alpine Club, eager to achieve the ascent of the mountain. Hinks, who had been seconded to the committee from his full-time post as secretary of the Royal Geographical Society, was an irascible and intolerant man, who lost no opportunity in furthering the interests of the geographers at the expense of the climbers. This frequently brought him into conflict with Percy Farrar, who strongly defended the climbing interests of the Alpine Club.

In mid-February George received a letter from Hinks requiring him to sign an agreement to be bound by the wishes of Charles Howard-Bury, the expedition's leader, and also to refrain from seeking any publicity, through the press or by writing a book, until after the publication of the official account of the expedition. Both these matters caused George considerable concern. He felt that once they reached the mountain he should be under the control of Howard Raeburn, as climbing leader. He was also worried over the ban on writing about the expedition. It was his intention to embark on a writing career when he returned home, and he felt that the proposed agreement was lacking in clarity. He also noted that it had no time limit. Hinks's reply showed little consideration for Mallory's worries, telling him to sign 'as others have' and giving him the bare assurance that he would be treated 'with every consideration'.

As time for the departure drew near George also began to feel doubts about the planning of the expedition. On 21 February he wrote to Geoffrey Young:

> I expect I shall have no cause to regret your persuasion in the cause of Mount Everest. At present, I'm highly elated at the prospect, and so is Ruth – thank you for that. My view about the party is chiefly that it is inadequate in numbers: there is no margin. Raeburn says he doesn't expect to get higher than about 24,000 to 25,000; Dr Kellas presumably will get no further; so the final part is left to Finch and me, and the outside chance that Wheeler or Morshead will take to climbing and make a success of it. Perhaps, after all, I shall be the weakest of the lot; but at present I feel more doubtful of Finch's health.

His feelings over George Finch were well founded. The climbers reported for their medicals in London on 17 March and shortly afterwards Finch was declared unfit to go. His medical report had in fact been inconclusive. Although he was basically in good health, his appearance was described as tired and sallow. He was slightly anaemic and had been losing weight. The doctors thought that he would probably improve considerably with training. Dr Wollaston, as the medical officer responsible for Finch's health on the mountain, had the final decision. He felt that he could not take the risk and recommended that a replacement be found. But there were no doubts about George. His report concluded :

> Height, 5ft 11ins; weight 11 stone 5 pounds. This man is in every respect fit.

There was now the urgent problem of finding a substitute for Finch. George was very worried when he heard the suggestion that William Ling, president of the Scottish Mountaineering Club, should be the replacement. He was forty-eight years old and his selection would leave George as the only young climber on the expedition. He expressed his fears to Arthur Hinks:

> I have been thinking very seriously of my own position. The substitution of Ling for Finch, though it may make little difference in the earlier stages of climbing, will in all probability very materially weaken the advance party. [...] For the final push we want men who can last. [...] I consider we ought to have another man who should be chosen not so much for his expert skill but simply for his powers of endurance. I have all along regarded the party as barely strong enough for a venture of this kind. [...] You will understand that I must look after myself in this matter. I'm a married man and I can't go into it bald-headed.

He received a typically brusque reply from Hinks:

> I don't think that you need feel under any anxiety about your own postion, because you will be under the orders of very experienced mountaineers who will take care not to call upon you for jobs that can't be done. The fact that you have been in close touch with Farrar all along has no doubt made you imbibe his view, which is hardly that of anybody else, that the first object of the expedition is to get to the top of Mount Everest this year.

In the event Ling wrote to the Everest Committee refusing the invitation. It was fortunate for George that at this juncture he heard that Guy Bullock, his old climbing friend from the Winchester Ice Club, who was now in the diplomatic service, had just returned to Britain on leave. On 31 March George wrote to Younghusband recommending that Bullock be chosen. He described him as a 'tough sort of fellow who never lost his head and would stand any amount of knocking about'. He added:

> He was a year junior to me and first came out to the Alps in 1905, my second season, with R.L.G. Irving, a Winchester master. He seemed to me then to have extraordinary stamina. He will almost certainly be available now. I feel that he would be a valuable member in the party, level-headed

and competent all round – a man in whom one would feel confident in
an emergency as one of the least likely of men to crack.

With the permission of the Foreign Secretary, Bullock was given a
special extension of his leave from the Foreign Office and was able
to join the expedition.

TEN

THE RECONNAISSANCE 1921

The expedition was planned to start from Darjeeling in mid-May. Morshead, Wheeler and Heron were already in India. So was Kellas, who was on his own expedition to the mountains of Sikkim. Raeburn left England in March to supervise the hiring of the porters, while Howard-Bury, Wollaston and Bullock sailed from Marseilles. George was the last to leave. He sailed from Tilbury on 8 April in the liner *Sardinia*, bringing with him the last consignment of expedition equipment. On the voyage he regularly ran around the deck to keep himself fit and he found a hidden corner in the bows were he could be alone and read *Martin Chuzzlewit* and Strachey's *Queen Victoria*. He also took part in deck games and joined a bridge school in the evening. The *Sardinia* docked at Calcutta on 9 May and, after completing arrangements for the transport of the equipment, George travelled north by train to Darjeeling, where he met the rest of the party at Government House. On 11 May a formal dinner was given in their honour by the Governor of Bengal. Dr Kellas arrived after the dinner had started. George took an immediate liking to him. As he told Ruth:

> Kellas I love already. He is beyond description Scotch and uncouth in his speech – altogether uncouth. He arrived at the great dinner party ten minutes after we had sat down, and very dishevelled, having walked in from Grom, a little place four miles away. His appearance would form an admirable model to the stage for a farcical representation of an alchemist.

He is very slight of build, short, thin, stooping, and narrow-chested; his head [...] made grotesque by veritable gig-lamps of spectacles and a long pointed moustache. He is an absolutely devoted and disinterested person.

The expedition left Darjeeling in two parties on 18 and 19 May. George was in the first group, with Howard-Bury, Wollaston and Wheeler, while Raeburn led the second party of Kellas, Bullock and Heron. The journey gave George the opportunity to evaluate the qualities of his companions. He found it difficult to establish a good relationship with the leader, Howard-Bury. As he told Ruth on 24 May:

He is not a tolerant person. He is well-informed and opinionated and doesn't at all like anyone else to know things he doesn't know. For the sake of peace, I am being very careful not to broach certain subjects of conversation. However, we are rubbing along quite well now. He knows a great deal about flowers and is very keen about them, and is often pleasant and sometimes amusing at meals.

George was more worried by the attitude of Raeburn, the climbing leader:

I saw, and still see, Raeburn as a great difficulty. He has some very tiresome qualities. He is very critical and unappreciative of other people in some ways. [...] He is evidently touchy about his position as leader of the Alpine party and wants to be treated with proper respect. And he is dreadfully dictatorial about matters of fact, and often wrong. It was very evident in Darjeeling that he would not get on with Howard-Bury, to say nothing of the rest of us, and in these circumstances I rather view myself as a soothing syrup. Luckily, I had a friendly little walk with Raeburn before we left Darjeeling and rather played up to his desire to give advice, so we get on very nicely. He has some very nice qualities; he has a good deal of fatherli-ness and kindliness, but his total lack of *calm* and of sense of humour at the same time is most unfortunate. I am rather sorry in a way that I am not with him now. I feel that he is a weak man whom it might be my good fortune to help.

Their route was planned to cross south-east Sikkim and enter Tibet by the Jelep La pass (14,390ft). On 5 June George sent Ruth a full description of their journey:

> To get into Tibet from Sikkim we had to cross a high pass, the Jelep La. [...] Most of the party rode ponies [...] but I made this an occasion for testing my wind, and found it quite as much as I wanted, and was tired and headachy on the descent.
>
> We went down to the Chumbi valley and afterwards followed it up to the tableland. It was a remarkable change of scenery from the moist and semitropical Sikkim to a much drier climate and a vegetation more like Europe, with pine and birch trees very prominent. The Chumbi valley in fact was not at all unlike many valleys in the Alps – only I doubt whether any Alpine valley can display such a variety of orchids, primulas, fritillaries, anemones, ranunculus, or such a mass of strawberry flower, to say nothing of rhododendrons, which cover the hillsides.
>
> The great change was coming up to the plains. [...] Nothing, I suppose, will ever be more dreary than the first stage from Phari: twenty-one miles mostly across an absolutely flat desert of gravel. The two fortunate circumstances were that the cruel wind was at our backs and that there were snow mountains to be looked at. It is no use pretending that mountains are always beautiful. Chomolhari (about 24,000ft) rising abruptly out of the plain to more than 9,000 feet above us, was certainly a very tremendous sight, astounding and magnificent; but in broad daylight, however much one may be interested by its prodigious cliffs, one is not charmed – one remains cold and rather horrified. But in the evening light this country can be beautiful, snow mountains and all: the harshness becomes subdued; shadows soften the hillsides; there is a blending of lines and folds until the last light, so that one comes to bless the absolute bareness, feeling that here is a pure beauty of form, a kind of ultimate harmony.

As they journeyed through Tibet it became clear that Dr Kellas was far from well. Two months earlier he had lost a stone in weight when climbing in Sikkim in severe conditions with inadequate food. He now developed enteritis, and he died on 5 June near Kampa Dzong. George was very distressed and wrote to David Pye:

He died without one of us anywhere near him, and yet it was a difficult position. The old gentleman (such he seemed) was obliged to retire
a number of times en route and could not bear to be seen in this distress,
and so insisted that everyone should be in front of him. Well, once one is
in front, one doesn't linger much in dusty places on the windswept plain;
and after our first anxieties none of us lingered much for Kellas. After all
there was nothing to be done for him if one did stay to see him, and he
didn't want it. [...] I know that I was deterred particularly on that last day
from staying behind by the feeling that I should be pushing into someone
else's business.

Dr Kellas was buried on a hillside just south of Kampa Dzong in sight
of the mountains he loved to climb. George expressed his feelings to
Geoffrey Young:

> It was an extraordinarily affecting little ceremony, burying Kellas on a stony
> hillside. [...] I shan't easily forget the four boys, his own trained mountain
> men, children of nature, seated in wonder on a great stone near the grave
> while Bury read out the passage from 1 Corinthians.

The party was now further weakened by the fact that before they left
Kampa Dzong Wollaston declared Harold Raeburn unfit to go on. He
had fallen twice from his horse and was suffering badly from diarrhoea.
Wollaston decided to return with him to Lachen in Sikkim, where he
could receive better medical attention. The difficulties confronting the
expedition now seemed immense. They were approaching unmapped
territory and the climbing party was reduced to two members, neither
of them with Himalayan experience.

As they set out from Kampa Dzong they suddenly had their first
view of Everest, a hundred miles away to the west. It was an exciting
moment and George wrote:

> There was no mistaking the two great peaks in the west: that to the left
> must be Makalu, grey, severe, and yet distinctly graceful, and the other away
> to the right – who could doubt its identity? It was a prodigious white fang
> excrescent from the jaw of the world.

A week later they obtained a second view of Everest, this time in sufficient detail to form some idea of the challenge ahead. George was quick
to observe what he described as 'two most notable cols to left and to right,
dividing the great mountain from its neighbours'. As he told Ruth:

> The problem of its great ridges and glaciers began to take shape and to haunt
> the mind, presenting itself at odd moments and leading to definite plans.

After arriving at Tingri Dzong, on 23 June George and Guy Bullock left
the main body of the expedition and set out to explore the northern
approaches to the mountain. They were accompanied by a cook and
sixteen porters under a sirdar. They entered the Rongbuk valley and after
two days suddenly caught their first sight of Everest from the north. It
was 16 miles away. George described what they saw:

> At the end of the valley and above the glacier Everest rises not so much a
> peak as a prodigious mountain mass. There is no complication for the eye.
> The highest of the world's great mountains, it seems, has to make but a
> simple gesture of magnificence to be lord of all, vast in unchallenged and
> isolated supremacy. To the discerning eye other mountains are visible, giants
> between 23,000 and 26,000 feet high. Not one of their slenderer heads even
> reaches their chief's shoulder; beside Everest they escape notice – such is
> the pre-eminence of the greatest.

Since any direct ascent of the north face was clearly out of the question, they pitched base camp just beyond the Rongbuk monastery and
spent the next four weeks exploring from the Rongbuk valley, searching
for a possible route to either of the two most notable cols which they
had observed. George found this work highly exciting. He told Ruth:

> My darling, this is a thrilling business altogether. I can't tell you how it
> possesses me, and what a prospect it is. And the beauty of it all!

After some days it became clear that the approach to the North Col
from the head of the Rongbuk glacier was impossibly steep. George
then thought that it might be possible to reach the South Col from a

great glacier basin which he had noticed on the far side of the west ridge and which, as a reminder of his beloved Welsh mountains, he named the Western Cwm. Striking up the West Rongbuk glacier, he and Bullock devoted all their energies to finding a way down into this basin. At last on 19 July, after many frustrations, they reached the col between Lingtren and Pumori, and were able to look down into the Western Cwm. George wrote in his diary:

> We reached the col at 5 a.m. a fantastically beautiful scene; and we looked across into the West Cwm at last, terribly cold and forbidding under the shadow of Everest.
>
> But another disappointment: it is a big drop, about 1,500ft down to the glacier, and a hopeless precipice. I was hoping to get away to the left and traverse into the cwm; that too is quite hopeless. However we have seen this western glacier and are not sorry we have not to go up it. It is terribly steep and broken. In any case, work on this side could only be carried out from a base in Nepal, so we have done with the western side.

They returned to base camp eager to leave the Rongbuk valley and explore the approach from the east, but now their plans received a sharp setback. George expressed his great disappointment to Ruth:

> I have had a bitter blow. All the photos taken up here with the quarter plate – practically all I have taken – have gone wrong. Apparently I put the plates in the wrong way round. I know nothing about plates and followed instructions given me by Heron. I have taken enormous trouble over these photos; many of them were taken at sunrise from places where neither I nor anyone else may go again.

There was nothing for it but to retrace their steps. Two days of frenetic activity followed, during which they made lightning raids with their cameras to the north and west. At last, on 25 July, after spending a month at high altitude, they were able to descend and to travel east to a new base at Kharta in the Arun valley.

They spent four days here, resting in delightful idleness. George told Ruth how much he enjoyed the change of scene:

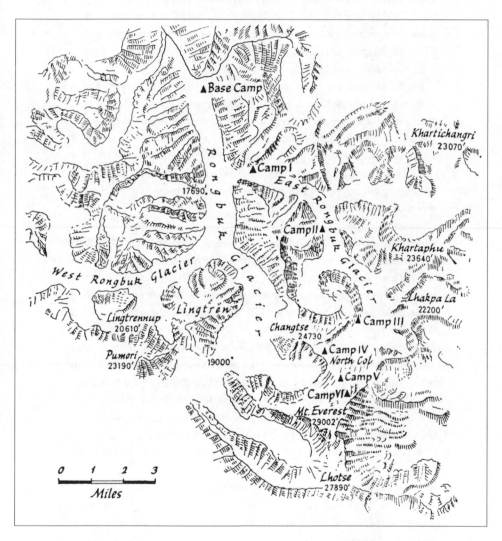

Map showing the northern approach to Everest, the Lhakpa La and the camps used on the 1922 and 1924 expeditions.

As we have come down lower, and nearer to the Arun valley, the appearance
of greenness has steadily increased. We have crossed two passes on the way,
and have slept near two clear bubbling streams; and all that we have seen
of snow mountains has been of interest, but none of that counts with me.
To see things grow again as they they liked growing, enjoying rain and sun
– that has been the real joy.

   I collected in a beautiful ramble a lovely bunch of wild flowers. The
commonest were a pink geranium and a yellow potentilla and a little flower
that looked for all the world like a violet but turned out from its leaf to be
something quite different; and there was grass of Parnassus, which I really
love, and in places a carpet of a little button flower, a brilliant pink, which I
think must belong to the garlic tribe. But most of all I was delighted to find
kingcups, a delicate variety rather smaller than ours at home, but somehow
especially reminding me of you.

On 2 August they were on the move again, hoping that the glacial
stream in the Kharta valley would provide a route to the North Col
from the east. After several days of frustrating reconnaissance, during
much of which time George was suffering from a feverish chill, it
became clear that this was not so. The glacier flowing from the North
Col, which they were so eager to reach, was separated from them by
an intervening ridge. On 18 August George and Bullock, now accompanied by Moreshead, summoning up all their energies for a supreme
effort, climbed to the Lhakpa La (22,200ft), the snow col on this ridge.
At last they could look down on to the glacier which ran from a cwm
under the north-east face of Everest. George was delighted to see that
there was an easy line of descent to the glacier and that the approach to
the North Col did not seem difficult. He wrote to Ruth in triumph:

We have found our way to the great mountain. [...] As we came down the
long, weary way, my thoughts were full of this prospect and this success.
I don't know when I have allowed myself so much enjoyment from a
personal achievement.

   Well my dear, that's the history of a day and also of a climax. [...] It is now
only a question of waiting for the weather and organising our push to the
summit. They say the monsoon should break at the end of this month and

the fine spell should set in with September. I hope it may. [...] Good night
and God bless you a thousand times, and Clare and Beridge and John.

They returned to their Kharta base camp for a rest, and plans were
made for a summit bid. Major Wheeler now arrived, having completed
a survey of the Rongbuk valley. He brought the surprising news that
the glacier flowing from the North Col, which they had so desperately
been trying to reach, in fact turned west and flowed through a narrow
valley which opened into the main Rongbuk glacier. If only they
had known this weeks before, what efforts would have been saved!
Bad weather and the need to retake many of their photographs had
prevented them from exploring this apparently small outlet. But there
was no question now of returning to the Rongbuk valley. They would
attempt to reach the North Col by way of the Lhakpa La.

On 31 August Mallory and Bullock moved to an advanced base
camp at 17,300ft, but bad weather then prevented any progress
for more than a fortnight. It is not surprising that, having spent so
long at high altitude and frustrated by the monsoon weather, some
tensions appeared in the party. George told Ruth of his feelings about
Howard-Bury:

> I've had trouble with him about stores – a most miserable petty business, so
> miserable I really can't bring myself to explain it. But his attitude amounted
> to an accusation of greed on my part in taking more than I ought up here
> for the use of the higher camps; and meanwhile B. and I are providing meat
> and tea for the coolies out of our own money, because we know they must
> be fed up and encouraged in this way if we are to get them up the mountain;
> and Bury will allow nothing outside their base rations.

George also confessed to Ruth that there were even tensions between
him and his friend Guy Bullock:

> We weren't getting on quite happily. We had rather drifted into that common
> superficial attitude between two people who live along together – competi-
> tive and slightly quarrelsome, each looking out to see that he doesn't get done
> down in some small way by the other. [...] We have even been eyeing the

food to see that the other doesn't take too much – horrible confession! But
a passage has happened between us to put it all right, or so I hope.

On 1 September, much to everyone's surprise, Howard Raeburn
turned up at base camp. He had made a difficult journey on his own
across Tibet and had been forced by serious flooding to make long
detours on the way. He seemed to have aged greatly since his illness
and his physical appearance was shocking. Although they greeted him
warmly enough, expedition members were angry to learn that on his
journey he had passed a consignment of mail for them but had made
no effort to pick it up. As Howard-Bury reported to Hinks:

> Raeburn turned up yesterday after a three month absence. He passed five
> bags of our mail at Chusar near Tinki and he made no attempt to bring
> them on! Can you imagine anyone being such a fool.

On 6 September Howard-Bury and Wollaston brought Raeburn up to
the mountain base camp. George was shocked at the deterioration in
him, and admitted to Geoffrey Young: 'When he is not being a bore I
feel moved to pity, but that is not often.' He was relieved that there was
now no question of Raeburn resuming the climbing leadership.
    The mail from England arrived on 9 September and included a letter
from Geoffrey Young urging that no foolish risks should be taken:

> The result is nothing compared to the rightness of the attempt. Keep it
> 'right' then; and let no desire for result spoil the effort by overstretching
> the safe limits within which it must move. [...] The summit may, in any
> particular case, lie outside the course. [...] Good fortune! and the 'resolution
> to return', even against ambition!

George's reply revealed the feelings of tension and anxiety which had
been building up during the weeks of hard effort:

> The excitement of the reconnaissance is all over. It was exciting, and we
> have found a good way to approach the mountain. That last push to a snow
> col which we had to see over was the biggest effort I have ever made on

a mountain. The whole thing is on my shoulders – I can say this to you. Bullock follows well and is safe; but you know what it means on a long, exhausting effort to lead all the time, and snow shoes in deep snow on a steep slope are no small added burden. [...]

Lord, how I wish you were here to talk it all over. It has been rather a strain, Geoffrey, altogether – both ways. I was unfortunate in having an attack of tonsillitis just before we finished our reconnaissance, and I feel somehow I'm not so strong as I was – less reserve, somehow. [...] I begin to feel that sort of malaise one has before putting a great matter, as it seems, to the touch. Geoffrey, at what point am I going to stop? It's going to be a fearfully difficult decision; there's an incalculable element about other men's physical condition, and all the more so under these strange conditions. I almost hope I shall be the first to give out!

He also expressed his doubts to Ruth:

The month is too late already for the great adventure. We shall have to face great cold, I've no doubt; and the longer the delay, the colder it will be. But the fine weather will come at last. My chance, the chance of a lifetime, I suppose, will be sadly shrunk by then.

On 16 September the weather cleared at last, and on the 22nd they established a camp at the Lhakpa La. On the next morning, George, Bullock and Wheeler, with ten Sherpas and supplies for three days, descended to the glacier (now named the East Rongbuk glacier) and placed a camp on the snowfield below the North Col. They endured a night of terrible winds which prevented any sleep, and set out at 7 a.m. They struggled up the great snow wall and after climbing for four and half hours reached the North Col just before midday. They scanned the north ridge carefully to see if a route was feasible. The angle was not very steep and there seemed to be easy rocks and snow all the way to the north-east crest. George later reported:

No obstacle appeared, or none so formidable that a competent party would not easily surmount it or go round it. If one harboured a doubt about this way before, it was impossible to keep it any longer.

But there was a savage wind sweeping across the north ridge and they had to take shelter under an ice-cliff.

> From top to bottom the ridge was exposed to the full fury of a gale from the northwest. [...] Under these circumstances the proper course for us was too clear. However, we decided to test the strength of the wind; and the three sahibs walked on 200 yards or so to the col itself. It was not a wind to blow one off the mountain; and by inclining the head at an angle away from it, it was possible to breathe even in the strongest gusts. But it was strong enough to leave no shadow of doubt in any of our minds. [...] I question whether anyone could have survived in it more than an hour or so.

They descended to their camp of the previous night. Wheeler now found that he had lost all sensation in both legs below the knees and it took George more than an hour's vigorous rubbing before the feeling was fully restored. Next morning they decided that they did not have the reserves to establish a camp at the North Col, as had been intended, and the decision was taken to retreat. They returned over the Lhakpa La and, after striking the upper camps, returned to Kharta. The expedition left for home on 5 October.

Although he was naturally disappointed not to get any higher, George felt proud of their achievement. He told Ruth:

> It is a disappointment, there is not getting over it, that the end should seem so much tamer than I had hoped. But it wasn't tame in reality; it was no joke getting to the North Col. I doubt if any big mountain venture has ever been made with a smaller margin of strength. [...] I had plenty of reserve personally and could have carried on another 2,000 feet anyway, with ease, had the conditions been favourable. As it is, we have established the way to the summit for anyone who cares to try the highest adventure.

He reserved his deepest feelings for Geoffrey Young:

> I think it was disappointment more than anything else that prevented me from writing before: the terrible difference between my visions of myself with a few determined spirits setting forth from our perched camp on that

high pass, crawling up at least to a much higher point where the summit itself would seem almost within reach, and coming down tired but not dispirited, satisfied rather, just with the effort; all that, and on the other hand the reality as we found it – the blown snow endlessly swept over the grey slopes, just the grim prospect, no respite, and no hope.

Well, that mood has passed long ago; and now [...] I'm conscious of the only feeling that's left: Thank God it was like that, with no temptation to go on.

Geoffrey Young's reply provided a fitting estimate of George's achievements:

This is to welcome you into quiet waters, in a very sincere spirit of relief, pride, and congratulation. You write [...] of 'failure'. You will find this end of the world is only using the word 'success' – unexpected, tremendously deserved, and beyond what we had hoped.

I can assure you that the colossal effort of lifting an entirely unsuitable party, at the first attempt, on a single pair of shoulders, not only on to the right line but well up it, against hopeless conditions, forms an episode by itself in the history of mountain exploration, and will only be the more appreciated as time goes on.

ELEVEN

PLANS FOR A SUMMIT BID 1922

George sailed from Bombay on the SS *Malwa* at the end of October and was reunited with Ruth in Marseilles on 12 November. It was eight months since he had last seen her and to celebrate their reunion they decided to stay at the Hotel Louvre et Paix, the finest and most expensive hotel in the city. But their freedom was to be short-lived. Awaiting George at the hotel was a letter from Sir Francis Younghusband inviting him to take part in a second Everest expedition in the following year:

> You seem all to be of opinion that May and June will be better months than September, so we are organising an expediton to start from Darjeeling on March 21st next year. We could not wait until 1923 because we cannot afford to lose the opportunity which the present friendliness of the Tibetans affords. [...] Also, the public interest in the Expedition is now so extraordinarily keen we could not allow it to cool. So we are very much hoping you will be able to go out again next year.

George had considerable misgivings about returning to Everest so soon. Before arriving in Marseilles he had written to his sister Avie:

> They've had thoughts of organising an expedition for next year; but I've said it's no use going out except early in the spring, to climb before the monsoon. They can't possibly organise another show so soon as I've also said that it's

barely worthwhile trying again, and anyway not without eight first-rate
climbers. They can't get eight, certainly not soon, perhaps not even the year
after. Hinks (Hon Sec) already wants to know whether I'll go again. When
they press for an answer, I shall tell them they can get the other seven first.....
I wouldn't go again next year, as the saying is, for all the gold in Arabia.

For a short period George left the matter open as he and Ruth spent
an enjoyable few days touring Provence. Eventually, after considering
the matter very carefully, they came to the consideration that he should
go out again. George felt that he simply could not refuse. Everest was
bringing him considerable fame. The committee had asked him to give
a series of lectures throughout Britain and it wanted him to write a
substantial section of the expedition book. He also felt that Everest
was in a sense unfinished business. He had established the way to the
North Col and he did not want any other climber to take over and
to complete the route to the summit. He wrote to Arthur Hinks to
clarify his position:

> I don't know precisely what I may have said in my haste from Marseilles
> but please don't tell the committee if the question arises that I don't intend
> to go unless they do as I wish. That's not my thought. I shall have to think
> that with so many chances against us we have some in our favour – but we
> can talk of that when we meet.

A few days after returning home, George had a meeting with Hinks
in London and agreed to take part in the 1922 expedition.

He had just three months in England between the two expeditions,
and Everest kept him busy for much of this time. On 10 January he
gave the first public lecture at the Queen's Hall and then travelled
widely around the country giving nearly thirty lectures. His performance was given wide coverage and earned much praise in the local
press. His lecture tour also had an encouraging financial outcome. The
Mount Everest Committee had said that he might keep 25 per cent
of the proceeds, and this share brought him a total of £400, which
was more than he would have earned in a year at Charterhouse. He
found lecturing an interesting experience and wrote:

I am much intrigued by the whole art of casting a spell on an audience; it's
rather amusing to practise one's guile on two or three thousand expectant
persons, but I wonder whether the experience will ever be related to anything
more useful in the future?

He also devoted much of this time to writing his contributions for the
1921 expedition book in which he described their attempts to find a
route on to the mountain and their progress as far as the North Col.

The specific aim of the 1922 expedition was to reach the summit
of the mountain, and a larger and much stronger climbing party was
chosen. As expected, Brigadier-General the Hon. Charles Bruce was
appointed expedition leader. He was an outstanding personality who
had served with Gurkha regiments for over thirty years, during which
time he had established a remarkable bond of loyalty and affection with
the men under his command. He treated them as younger members
of his own family and made outrageous jokes with them in their own
language. He was a larger-than-life character. When he was stationed
near the Khyber Pass he was reputed to have carried his orderly up a
hill every day to improve his fitness and he was renowned for intro-
ducing shorts into the British Army. Now aged fifty-five, he was not
expected to climb much above base camp and his role would be that
of planning the strategy for the assault and maintaining the morale of
the team as a cohesive unit. Aware of the penny-pinching attitude of
the committee secretary Arthur Hinks, he was also fully determined
to spend whatever was necessary to ensure the team's success.

Lieutenant-Colonel Edward Strutt was appointed his deputy and
leader of the climbing party. A soldier and a diplomat, he had once
been the High Commissioner in Danzig and had more than thirty
years' experience of climbing in the Alps. Although an opinionated
man and a stickler for tradition, he proved himself popular on the
expedition as he regaled his companions with tales from his military career, including the memorable occasion in 1919 when he had
rescued the Austrian imperial family from a revolutionary mob and
escorted them to sanctuary in Switzerland. Aged forty-eight, he was
not expected to take part in a summit bid but would direct the activities of the climbing group from their mountain base camp.

The climbing party consisted of five members: George Mallory, George Finch, Howard Somervell, Arthur Wakefield and Edward Norton. George Finch had overcome the disappointment of his rejection in the previous year by making some fine ascents in the Alps, and when examined by two doctors in November had been declared absolutely fit. Howard Somervell was a powerfully built surgeon from Kendal in the Lake District. After a double-first at Cambridge and distinguished medical service during the war, he later turned his back on an eminent surgical career to work as a medical missionary in Travancore in South India. Aged thirty-two, he was a fine alpine climber and had completed an outstanding season in the previous year, climbing over thirty peaks. Arthur Wakefield, who like Somervell came originally from Kendal and was also a doctor, had been a keen fell-runner in his youth and had achieved some remarkable rock climbs in the Lake District. He was now living in Canada and he sold his medical practice in order to come on the expedition. Edward Norton was the grandson of Sir Alfred Wills, who had made the first ascent of the Wetterhorn in 1854, which is usually regarded as marking the beginning of mountaineering as a sport. He was a keen climber and was also devoted to polo and pig-sticking (wild boar hunting on horseback). He was a modest and cultured man and had the advantage of speaking several Hindi dialects.

Dr Tom Longstaff was appointed the official doctor to the expedition and also its naturalist. He had considerable experience of Himalayan climbing, but at the age of forty-seven he was expected to act only in a support role. He was a small, wiry man and at his medical examination the doctors unkindly described him as 'not a very good specimen'. He had a wry sense of humour and before the expedition left England he jocularly told its members:

> I want to make one thing clear. I am the expedition's official medical officer. And I am, as a matter of a fact, a qualified doctor, but I feel it my duty now to remind you that I have never practised in my life. I beg you in no circumstances to seek my professional advice, since it would almost certainly turn out to be wrong. I am however willing if necessary to sign a certificate of death.

John Noel, who had long dreamed of going to Everest and had made
that secret journey into Tibet in 1913, was appointed the expedition photographer. Younghusband had hoped that an artist might
also accompany the expedition 'to paint the greatest peaks of the
Himalaya'. But none of the artists under consideration were able to
pass the medical examination. This task was therefore left to Howard
Somervell, who was a talented amateur artist.

Much greater attention was given to the supply of suitable clothing
and equipment for the expedition than had been the case in 1921. The
climbers were equipped with specially designed clothing including
woollen waistcoats, Jaeger pants, windproof cotton smocks and a range
of footwear. Improvements were made to the tents and the bedding.
Bruce also insisted that a greater variety of food should be provided,
with the result that such luxuries as crystallised ginger and quails in
truffles were included.

There was much discussion over whether the use of oxygen would
improve the performance of the climbers. There was a growing aware-
ness of the difficulties of climbing at high altitudes and in January a
sub-committee was set up to conduct tests and to assess the potential
value of using oxygen. After receiving their report, the Mount Everest
Committee took the revolutionary decision to supply the high climbers with oxygen. They allocated £400 for the provision of ten oxygen
sets and a large number of metal cylinders containing compressed
oxygen. George Finch, who had taken a keen interest in the problems
of high-altitude climbing and had served on the sub-committee, was
appointed the expedition's oxygen officer. The decision to take oxygen
sparked off a bitter controversy. Some regarded it as an artificial aid
and considered that to use it to climb Everest would not be legitimate
mountaineering. Arthur Hinks, never one to avoid a controversy, after
hearing that the supplier of the equipment had given the instruction
that oxygen should be used continuously above 23,000ft, expressed
his feelings in a letter to Percy Farrar:

> I should be especially sorry if the oxygen outfit prevents them going as high
> as possible without it. [...] If some of the party do not go to 25,000–26,000ft
> without oxygen, they will be rotters.

Farrar swiftly retorted:

> Strictly speaking, I do not think that oxygen is any more of an artificial aid
> than food. The human frame is attuned to a certain supply of oxygen. All we
> have endeavoured to do is to make up the supply to the normal quantity.

George's initial reaction was against the use of oxygen. He believed
that a process of gradual acclimatisation to altitude and the use of a
deep-breathing technique which he had adopted in 1921 would be
equally effective. As he told David Pye:

> When I think of mountaineering with four cylinders of oxygen on one's
> back and a mask over one's face – well, it loses its charm.

General Bruce travelled to India ahead of the main party in order
to supervise the transport arrangements. On his arrival he appointed
two Gurkha officers, his nephew, Captain Geoffrey Bruce, and Captain
John Morris, as transport officers for the expedition. To assist them he
enlisted Colin Crawford of the Indian Civil Service, who was also an
experienced climber. In addition he approached the Survey of India and
secured the release of Major Henry Morshead. By these means Bruce
considerably strengthened the climbing potential of the team without
making any reference to the Everest Committee in London. He also
arranged for suitable gifts to be taken to ensure the co-operation of the
Tibetan officials they would meet, and commented:

> I am taking brocade for the Rongbuk Lama, and twenty-four Homberg
> hats – the nearest way to the heart of all subordinate officials.

The expedition sailed from England on 2 March on board the
SS *Caledonia*. Although George enjoyed the company of his fellow
climbers, he developed the habit of rising very early in the morning
to have the deck to himself for what he called 'seasoned silence'. He
played deck tennis with Somervell and Wakefield, and, after attending
Finch's oxygen class, he overcame some of his earlier reservations about
its use. They landed at Bombay and, after a tiring train journey across

India, the expedition left Darjeeling in two groups on 26 March. The
expedition support team included forty climbing porters, eight photographic porters, ten oxygen porters, a sirdar (leader of the porters),
an interpreter, a cobbler, a tent-repairer and several first-class cooks. As
Bruce commented to Hinks, 'the outfit is rather tremendous'.

Although George felt the repetition of the long journey into Tibet
a rather tedious affair, he found the company of the other members
of the expedition highly congenial and he regarded General Bruce's
leadership as 'absolutely splendid'. On 26 April he wrote to Ruth
from Shekar Dzong:

> It is happening very much as it happened before. One starts in the crisp
> sunny air, generally about 7.30 a.m. or 8.00 at the latest. [...] As a rule one
> walks for a good stretch at the start. Perhaps half a dozen joining up in
> some sandy spot for tiffin (cheese and biscuits and chocolate) and later flog
> our tired animals along the last weary miles into camp. Our enormous mess
> tent has usually preceded us and is waiting at the end of our day's march
> to provide a welcome shelter when we come in. [...] A usual and by now
> a welcome sound in each new place is Strutt's voice, cursing Tibet – this
> march for being more dreary and repulsive even than the one before, and
> this village for being more filthy than any other. Not that Strutt is precisely
> a grouser; but he likes to ease his feelings with maledictions and, I hope
> feels better for it.
>
> I suppose in the last analysis it is not a time of active interest with me.
> I keep sufficiently interested, one way or another, to keep my head above
> water; but I function in a sort of undertone. Life seems more of an endur-
> ance and a waiting than an active doing of things that seem worth while.

Clockwise from top left:

31 Sir George Everest, Surveyor-General of India 1823–43.

32 Dr Alexander Kellas.

33 Percy Farrar, who represented the Alpine Club on the Mount Everest Committee.

34 The members of the 1921 expedition. From left to right, standing: Wollaston, Howard-Bury, Heron, Raeburn. Sitting: Mallory, Wheeler, Bullock, Morshead.

35 George Mallory's photograph of Everest from their 20,000ft camp, taken on the last day before they withdrew from the mountain in 1921.

36 Members of the 1922 expedition. From left to right, back row: Morshead, Geoffrey Bruce, Noel, Wakefield, Somervell, Morris, Norton. Front row: Mallory, Finch, Longstaff, General Bruce, Strutt, Crawford.

37 *Left:* General Bruce drinking chang (native beer) on the way to Tibet.

38 *Below:* Edward Norton.

39 *Right:* Howard
Somervell.

40 *Below:* Base Camp
and Everest in evening
light, 1922.

41 Camp IV on the North Col.

42 The members who took part in the first assault on the summit, 21 May 1922. From left to right: Morshead, Mallory, Somervell, Norton.

43 Mallory and Norton approaching their highest point, 26,995ft, 21 May 1922.

44 The summit of Everest seen from 26,995ft, the highest point reached by Mallory, Norton and Somervell, 21 May 1922.

45 George Mallory.

46 *Opposite:* Andrew Irvine.

47 *Right:* George and Andrew Irvine on board the SS *California*.

48 *Below:* The members of the 1924 expedition. From left to right, standing: Irvine, Mallory, Norton, Odell, MacDonald (the trade agent). Sitting: Shebbeare, Geoffrey Bruce, Somervell, Beetham.

49 *Left:* Noel Odell.

50 *Below:* Andrew Irvine outside the tent which he used as a workshop for improving the oxygen apparatus.

51 Mallory (left) and Irvine about to leave Camp IV, 6 June 1924.

Dear Noel
    We'll probably start early to-morrow (8th) in order to have clear weather. It won't be too early to start looking out for us either crossing the rockband under the pyramid or going up skyline at 8.0 p.m.

    Yr. ever
        G Mallory

52 Mallory's note to John Noel.

53 The memorial cairn erected at Base Camp in 1924 to those who had died on the first three Everest expeditions.

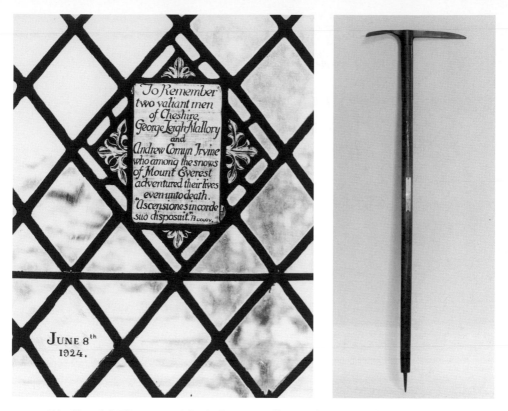

54 *Above left:* The memorial window to Mallory and Irvine in the South Cloister of Chester Cathedral.

55 and 56 *Above right and below:* The ice axe found on Everest in 1933.

57 and 58 George's son John, together with his wife Jennifer and their son George, at Base Camp in May 1995 for the dedication of a new memorial plaque in memory of George Mallory, Andrew Irvine and all those who died on the early British expeditions.

TWELVE

THE ASSAULT 1922

The expedition arrived at the Rongbuk monastery on 30 April. According to the plan devised by Charles Bruce they would go up the East Rongbuk Glacier to the ice basin below the North Col. After climbing to the North Col they would aim for the north-east ridge and make their summit bid from there. Six camps would be established along the route. Three would be placed along the East Rongbuk Glacier, one on the North Col at 23,000ft, and the final two at 25,000ft and 27,000ft.

On 1 May base camp was pitched just below the foot of the main glacier, and by 12 May three camps had been sited on the East Rongbuk glacier. After establishing the route from Camp III to the North Col, Mallory and Somervell remained several days at Camp III for the build-up to the first ascent. There was not much to do but they spent the time agreeably together, playing picquet, reading aloud to each other and talking about poetry. Somervell has left his impression of this time alone with George:

> When one shares a tent for days on end [...] with a man, one gets an insight into his character such as is vouchsafed to few other men. These many days of companionship with a man whose outlook on life was lofty and choice, human and loving [...] still remain for me a priceless memory. I forget the details of George Mallory's views on most of the many subjects we discussed, but in general he took always the big and liberal view. He was

really concerned with social evils, and recognised that they could only be
satisfactorily solved by the changing and ennobling of individual character.
He hated anything that savoured of hypocrisy and humbug, but cherished
all that is really good and sound.

The original plan had been for Mallory and Somervell, climbing without oxygen, to make the first summit bid, while Finch and
Norton later made a second attempt using oxygen sets. On 16 May
Strutt, accompanied by Morshead and Norton, arrived at Camp III
with news of a change of plan. Finch was suffering from dysentery
and Bruce, influenced by continuing doubts about the wisdom of
using oxygen, had decided to add Norton and Morshead to the first
attempt. This change of plan had some serious disadvantages. The
porters would have to carry twice as much equipment up to the
North Col to establish Camp IV. As a result, they would only be
able to establish one higher camp, at about 26,000ft, instead of the
two originally planned. It also meant that when Finch recovered his
health he would be left without a lead climber to accompany him on
a second summit attempt.

On 17 May Camp IV was established on a terrace close to the
North Col, and the first summit attempt was planned for two days
later. In a letter to Ruth, George assessed their chances of success:

> I write to you on the eve of our departure for the highest we can reach, just
> because I shall feel happier, in case of difficulties, to think that I have sent
> you a message of love. The difficulties will be such as we know, in all prob-
> ability; our endurance and will to go on taking precautions are less known
> factors. But with such good people as these I feel sure that we shall all be
> anxious to help each other. [...] Well, it's all on the knees of the gods, and
> they are bare cold knees. We shan't get to the top; if we reach the shoulder
> at 27,400 it will be better than anyone here expects.
>
> Dearest one, you must know that the spur to do my best is you and you
> again. In moments of depression or lack of confidence or overwhelming
> fatigue, I want more than anything to prove worthy of you. All my love to
> you. Many kisses to Clare and Beridge and John.

The 19th was a fine sunny day and at 8.45 a.m. the summit party of Mallory, Somervell, Norton and Morshead, together with nine Sherpas, set out for Camp IV. In his report for *The Times* George described their feelings of optimism:

> Domestic activities occupied the afternoon; and, when the sun left us at 4.30 p.m., we turned in for the night, all well fed and comfortable enough and proud in the possession of six thermos flasks filled with water for the morning meal. Our prospects seemed extraordinarily promising. It was our intention to carry on next morning only four loads: two of the smallest tents, two double sleeping-bags, food for one and a half days, our cooking pots and two thermos flasks. For this purpose, we had nine coolies, now well housed by threes in Mummery tents, so that we should have two coolies for each load and even so a margin of one. Everything had been arranged so happily and satisfactorily that one could hardly doubt these men would be able to establish our camp a great deal higher up the mountain next day.

Next morning, however, all nine Sherpas were suffering from mountain sickness, and only five were eventually fit to continue. After a late start they found progress difficult in a biting wind. After stopping to put on extra clothing a careless flick of the rope by Mallory knocked Norton's rucksack from his lap and sent it flying down the mountain. They continued to make slow progress and were only able to reach 25,000 feet before establishing Camp V. George's report described their situation:

> There was no visible camping place where we were. We traversed round on the sheltered side, vaguely hoping that one would appear. Eventually the coolies, with Somervell, professed to have found the right place. On the steep mountainside they proceeded to build a wall and so eventually to construct a comparatively flat place for one Mummery tent. Norton and I, in feeble imitation of their efforts, proceeded to select another place; but somehow our walls wouldn't work. One site after another was a failure, until we eventually found a steep slab which at all events was a secure piece of ground, and here ultimately pitched our tent in such a way that the slab was half our floor.

No more uncomfortable arrangement could have been devised, for the inevitable result must be to push one man down upon the other as they lay, and squeeze them tight together, so as to increase to agony the pain of sharp rocks forming the other parts of the floor. There, at all events, were the two little tents, perched fifty yards apart in some sort of fashion for security on the rocks, containing each a double sleeping-sack for a night's warmth in that cold place, and soon to contain the hopes of a day's mountaineering unlike all others from the mere fact that we should start from a point on the earth's surface higher than any reached before.

They set out at about 8 a.m. Morshead, who was feeling unwell, decided not to accompany them. The conditions were unfavourable: fresh snow covered the awkwardly tilting ledges and concealed loose stones, and their progress was slow. George recalled:

We had for a long time good hopes of reaching the northeast shoulder; but the long descent had to be borne in mind, and the retarding circumstance of fresh snow. It was agreed that we should turn back not much later than two o'clock. At 2.15 we reached, as it were, a head of rocks still 600 or 700ft below the northeast ridge of the mountain and commanding a clear view from here to the summit. The pace of the party had become extremely slow. There was obvious risk in going much farther; and greatly as we desired to gain the shoulder (there is no doubt that we were physically capable of getting there), the only wisdom was now in retreat. The aneroid registered 26,800 feet.

They retraced their steps and by 4 p.m. had reached their high camp of the previous night where they were welcomed by Morshead. After gathering up a few belongings they continued their descent along a ledge they had followed the day before. Freshly fallen snow made their progress difficult and they were nearly overwhelmed by disaster. Morshead, who was completely exhausted, suddenly slipped from his foothold and began pulling Somervell and Norton with him. Somervell later described what happened:

I was going last, and Mallory first, at a place were we had to cross the steep head of a long, wide couloir which swept down to the foot of the mountain, 3000 feet below us. The man in front of me slipped at a time when I was just moving myself, and I, too, was jerked out of my steps. Both of us began sliding at increasing speed down the icy couloir. The second man checked our progress for a moment, but could not hold us. He, too, was dragged off his feet. But Mallory had had just enough time to prepare for a pull on the rope, digging his axe firmly into the hard snow. It held, and so did the rope, and the party was saved. [...] Mallory had saved my life and the lives of us all.

In his report for *The Times* George contented himself with the brief statement : 'A nasty slip occurred, and three men were held by a rope belayed over the head of an ice-axe.' But writing to Ruth he commented:

The slip was nearly a bad business. I hadn't realised then how shaky Morshead was and had cut rather poor steps; but there was good holding for the pick. Norton and Somervell must have been caught napping. I hadn't the rope belayed round my axe, as I was on the point of cutting a step, but, hearing something wrong behind, drove in my pick and belayed and was ready in plenty of time when the strain came.

George's report vividly highlights the continuing difficulties of their descent:

The party proceeded with great caution after this incident, and it soon became evident that we should be racing against darkness. When we regained the great snow ridge, no trace of our upward steps appeared. The cutting of steps had now to be repeated; and the grim slow process was observed about 6.00 p.m. by Strutt below in Camp III. [...] Morshead, though he had been climbing in the pluckiest fashion, with tremendous efforts of breathing, had now come to the end of his tether. At best, he could proceed but a few steps at a time. Fortunately, it was easy going all the way down to the North Col as we watched the diminishing light. Norton supported Morshead on his shoulder while I found the easiest way down and Somervell brought up the rear. Sinister grey clouds away to the west, and some flickering lightning, after the sun had set over one of the most amazing of mountain views, seemed full of malice. What sort of a wind should we find on the Col after dark, when our difficulties were due to begin again?

By good fortune or good providence, when the moment arrived and the dimly starlit crevasses confronted us, Somervell produced a lantern from his rucksack; and so calm was the air that even a Japanese match, after a dozen trials or so, was found to light the candle. We groped a little to find our way, but no one had fallen through the surface before we reached the edge of a little cliff. Here it was necessary to jump about twelve feet down into the snow – a sufficiently alarming prospect at that hour. But the leap was safely accomplished. One fixed rope, if we could find it, would take us down to our terrace – the terrace where we had seen our five tents still neatly pitched in a row, awaiting our arrival. The rope was buried in snow, and the last of our candle burnt out. We groped for some time along the edge of the precipice and then began to go down a steep slope, in some doubt as to whether this were the way. Suddenly someone hooked up the rope from under the snow. We knew then that we could reach our tents.

But a terrible disappointment awaited them. Although there was plenty of food the porters had taken all the cooking pots and the fuel down to Camp III. As Somervell commented: 'We were so indescribably thirsty that to eat a single morsel of food without a drink was unthinkable.' George described the solution adopted by Norton:

He opened a tin of jam and a tin of milk, and mixed these in a mug with snow. I followed his example. The result he thought delicious; to me it seemed disgusting, but at least it could be swallowed.

They descended to Camp III the next day. It was a laborious journey: they had to cut steps most of the way under a hot sun, and what might have been expected to take one hour in fact took four. They were met by George Finch and Geoffrey Bruce carrying two thermos flasks of hot tea. Somervell described their feelings of relief:

We all arrived at Camp III alive – but with what a thirst! For thirty-six hours we had been struggling and panting in a dry, cold climate, losing pints of water from our lungs, and without any drink to repair the deficiency. I have never been so thirsty in my life; they tell me that I had seventeen large cups of tea without stirring from my seat.

Finch had recovered from his attack of dysentery and had arrived at Camp II on 18 May, accompanied by Geoffrey Bruce, Wakefield and a Gurkha named Tejbir. He spent that afternoon giving Bruce and Tejbir, who were both novices at mountaineering, lessons in the use of the ice axe so that they could accompany him in a second attempt on the summit, and on the next day they went up to Camp III. They spent the next three days overhauling all their equipment and checking their stores of oxygen. They also went for several trial walks from the camp and Finch was delighted to note that he and Bruce using oxygen easily outpaced Strutt and Wakefield who were accompanying them. On 22 May they climbed to the North Col to assist the first summit party in their descent, and two days later they went up to Camp IV to make their own attempt on the summit.

On 25 May, using oxygen, they established their high camp at 25,500ft, but were then imprisoned for twenty-four hours by a violent blizzard. During the second night, tired and weak through lack of food, they nearly succumbed to the numbing cold. Suddenly Finch remembered the oxygen. Bringing a set into the tent he soon had a flow going and warmth was restored to their frozen limbs. On the next day they set out at 6.30 a.m. but Tejbir was only able to climb about 500ft before returning to the tent. Finch and Bruce continued and reached a new record height of 27,200 feet before they were forced to turn back after trouble developed in Bruce's oxygen apparatus. Despite the failure of their attempt Finch reckoned that he had sufficiently demonstrated the advantages of using oxygen. He calculated that with its aid he had climbed at a rate of 1,000ft an hour, compared with Mallory's average of 300ft.

All the members of the expedition now gathered at Base Camp to recuperate. Most had suffered from their exertions. George had a temporary heart thrill and frostbitten fingers, and Longstaff considered that, apart from Somervell, no climber was fit to continue. But General Bruce was being constantly bombarded by letters from both Hinks and Younghusband that he should do everything in his power to reach the summit. Younghusband even suggested that if necessary the party should remain until after the monsoon. Reluctantly Bruce agreed that a third summit attempt should be made, by Mallory, Somervell and Finch. Although he was pleased to be included in the party, George had some misgivings about another attempt, as he told David Pye:

> David, it's an infernal mountain, cold and treacherous. Frankly the game is not good enough: the risks of getting caught are too great; the margin of strength when men are at great heights is too small. Perhaps it's mere folly to go up again. But how can I be out of the hunt?

And writing to Ruth he said:

> No doubt you will have mixed feelings about another venture, but you will feel chiefly as I do that it would have been unbearable for me to be left out. [...] The finger is far from well, and I risk getting worse frostbite by going up again, but the game is worth a finger, and I shall take every conceivable care.

They started from Base Camp on 3 June but, after arriving at Camp I, Finch, who was clearly unfit from his previous exertions, withdrew from the party. Heavy snow prevented them setting out on the next day and when they arrived at Camp III on the 5th they decided to make use of oxygen. Mallory and Somervell started for the North Col at 8 a.m. on 7 June, accompanied by Crawford and fourteen porters. They were aware that the recent heavy fall of snow might make the final steep slope up to the North Col liable to avalanche and Somervell outlined the precautions they took:

> At 10.15 we started the ascent of the snowy slopes of the North Col, which are steepest near their lowest part. Here we considered it most likely that an avalanche would occur. We tried to start one by stamping and jerking and threading out long trenches across the slope. But the snow would not budge, and we put all thoughts of such a possibility from our minds.

They were about 600ft below the Col when disaster struck. George described to Ruth what happened:

> I was following up in the steps, last on our rope of four, when at 1.50 I heard a noise not unlike an explosion of untamped gunpowder. I had never before been near an avalanche of snow, but I knew the meaning of that noise as though I were accustomed to hear it every day. In a moment I observed the snow's surface broken only a few yards away to the right and instinctively moved in that direction. And then I was moving downward.
>
> Somehow I managed to turn out from the slope so as to avoid being pushed headlong and backwards down it. For the briefest moment my chances seemed good, as I went quietly sliding down with the snow. Then the rope at my waist tightened and held me back. A wave of snow came over me. I supposed that the matter was settled. However I thrust out my arms to keep them above the snow and at the same time tried to raise my back, with the result that, when after a few seconds the motion stopped, I felt little pressure from the snow and found myself on the surface.

After extricating himself George found that Somervell and Crawford were safe, but only five of the porters could be seen. They soon realised that two ropes of porters, one of five and one of four, had been swept over the edge of a 60ft ice-cliff just below them. They hurried to the foot of this cliff and managed to dig out two men alive, but the remaining seven had been killed by their fall. In accordance with the wishes of their companions they left the dead porters buried in the snow where they had fallen. A large cairn to their memory was constructed at Camp III and the expedition withdrew from the mountain.

George sailed for England on 5 August, much burdened by thoughts of the accident. He wrote to Ruth:

> It's difficult to get it all straight in my mind. The consequences of my mistake are so terrible; it seems almost impossible to believe that it has happened for ever and that I can do nothing to make good. There is no obligation I have so much wanted to honour as that of taking care of these men. They are children where mountain dangers are concerned, and they do so much for us; and now through my fault seven of them have been killed.

He also expressed his feelings of responsibility to Sir Francis Younghusband:

> I'm very much to blame for this terrible accident, and I'm very sorry. I want you to believe that it was not the result of any spirit of recklessness or any carelessness of coolies' lives. If I had known more about snow conditions here, the accident would not have happened, and so one may say it was due to ignorance. [...] I am particularly sorry for the loss of these men. They had done remarkably well.

Younghusband sent a kindly reply, in which he said that, however much George might blame himself: 'I certainly am not one to blame you, for I have done precisely the same thing myself in the Himalaya, and only the purest luck can have saved me and my party from disaster.' And, in a letter to Hinks, General Bruce also expressed his sympathy: 'I am very sorry for Mallory, as he genuinely took great interest in all the porters and was generally very upset.'

Other members of the expedition also expressed their views about the accident. Strutt, who was by now in England, wrote George a sympathetic letter:

> I am awfully sorry for you, and I know well how much you are feeling this disaster. You ask me for comments – well I will not criticise from a distance. [...] I will add, if you will allow me, that after the great fall of fresh snow, seventeen persons on the North Col was fifteen too many, even after two days perfect weather. Don't think these are criticisms; the man on the spot must be the sole judge, and he gets the reward or pays the penalty.

Longstaff in a letter to Wollaston was more forthright in his criticism. After complaining that the Everest Committee:

> had consistently treated Bruce meanly; had not appreciated his difficulties: had quite unnecessarily and most ungenerously urged him to repeated attacks on the peak and hence had landed us in an accident which made us all feel horribly humiliated...

he concluded:

> To attempt such a passage in the Himalaya after new snow is idiotic. What
> the hell did they think they could do on Everest in such conditions, even
> if they did get up the North Col?

George also received a characteristically sympathetic note from
Geoffrey Young:

> Put entirely out of your mind that anyone has ever thought of placing
> any responsibility for the accident on you or the mountaineers. [...] You
> see, we *knew*; we were impressed throughout by the enormous percent-
> age of 'chance' in such climbing. If in the Alps we admitted it existed,
> in such an attempt it loomed indefinably great. [...]
>
> You made all the allowance for the safety of your party that your experi-
> ence suggested. [...] The immense percentage of chance or we may call it
> of the unknown, present still in this hitherto unattempted region of moun-
> taineering, turned for once against you. Well? What then? You took your full
> share, a leading share in the risk. In the war we had to do worse: we had to
> *order* men into danger at times when we could not share it. [...]
>
> It has been a great and very gallant attempt, and has accomplished far
> more that I for one ever expected.

The tragic end to the expedition had a profound effect on George.
He had always been well aware of the dangers inherent in mountaineering, and had known several of his friends to be killed in the
mountains, but this was the first time he himself had been involved in
a fatal accident. He felt it the more deeply because the people who
had died had been those for whom he was responsible. He shared the
attitude of Somervell, who later wrote:

> I remember well the thought gnawing at my brain. 'Only Sherpas and
> Bhotias killed – why, oh why could not one of us Britishers have shared
> their fate?' I would gladly at that moment have been lying there dead in
> the snow, if only to give those fine chaps who had survived the feeling that
> we had shared in their loss, as we had indeed shared the risk.

Later, when writing his chapters for the 1922 expedition book, in a remarkable piece of sustained writing, in one long sentence George expressed his mixed feelings over the whole venture and his admiration for the untamed nature of Mount Everest:

It is true that I did what I could to reach the summit, but now as I look back and see all those wonderful preparations, the great array of boxes collected at Phari Dzong and filling up the courtyard of the bungalow, the train of animals and coolies carrying our baggage across Tibet, the thirteen selected Europeans so snugly wrapt in their woollen waistcoats and Jaeger pants, their armour of wind-proof materials, their splendid overcoats, the furred finneskoes or felt-sided boots or fleece-lined moccasins devised to keep warm their feet, and sixty strong porters with them delighting in underwear from England and leathern jerkins and puttees from Kashmir; and then, unforgettable scene, the scatter of our stores at the Base Camp, the innumerable neatly-made wooden boxes concealing the rows and rows of tins – of Harris's sausages, Hunter's hams, Heinz's spaghetti, herrings *soi-disant* fresh, sardines, sliced bacon, peas, beans, and a whole forgotten host besides, sauce-bottles for the Mess tables, and the rare bottles more precious than these, the gay tins of sweet biscuits, Ginger Nuts and Rich Mixed, and all the carefully chosen delicacies; and besides all these for our sustenance or pleasure, the fuel supply, uncovered in the centre of the camps, green and blue two-gallon cans of paraffin and petrol, and an impressive heap of yak-dung; and the climbing equipment – the gay little tents with crimson flies or yellow, pitched here only to be seen and admired, the bundles of soft sleeping bags, soft as eiderdown quilt can be, the ferocious crampons and other devices, steel-pointed and terrible, for boots' armament, the business-like coils of rope, the little army of steel cylinders containing oxygen under high pressure, and not least, the warlike sets of apparatus for using the life-giving gas; and lastly, when I call to mind the whole begoggled crowd moving with slow determination over the snow and up the mountain slopes and with such remarkable persistence bearing up the formidable loads, when after the lapse of months I envisage the whole prodigious evidences of this vast intention, how can I help rejoicing in the yet undimmed splendour, the undiminished glory, the unconquered supremacy of Mount Everest?

THIRTEEN

LECTURER: BRITAIN AND AMERICA 1923

George arrived home in the middle of August. For the next six weeks he managed to spend time alone with his family. He bought a car, a 1.5-litre Albert, and went with Ruth on a holiday to France. By mid-October, however, he found himself committed to Everest business once more. Planning had begun for another expedition in 1924 and the committee was anxious to raise funds towards the expenses. They negotiated arrangements for an extensive lecture programme with Gerald Christie, the agent who had acted for them in 1921. Christie advised against the suggestion made by Hinks that as many members of the expedition as possible should take part:

> I think it would be wisest if one, or perhaps two, of the actual climbing party were deputed by the committee to be, so to speak, the 'star' lecturers for the big centres. [...] It may seem invidious to make distinctions, but from my own feelings in the matter and from what I gather from conversation with people generally, Mr Mallory and Captain Finch are to two who stand out most prominently in the minds of the public and would seem to me to be the two who should be 'starred'. We all know Mr Mallory can speak well and I happen to know that Captain Finch is most effective on the lecture platform and can tell a story admirably.

And in a postscript he added:

Mr Mallory would do big things in America. Our representative over there
is very anxious to have him go as soon after Xmas as convenient.

An extensive lecture tour was arranged. Each lecture centre was
allowed to choose which of the two main speakers they wanted, and it
turned out that Mallory and Finch were equally in demand. After the
joint meeting of the Alpine Club and the Royal Geographical Society
in London on the 16 October, they gave over fifty lectures between
them, covering all the major centres of the country. Despite the tragic
end to the 1922 expedition there was great public interest in Everest
and they found themselves speaking to packed audiences. Once again
George's income from three months of lecturing amounted to more
than his former Charterhouse salary for a year, and he also earned
extra money writing articles on Everest.

Plans were now drawn up for George to make a three-month
lecture tour of the USA. On Christie's advice the Everest Committee
decided to use the services of Mr Lee Keedick of New York as
manager for the tour. In January 1923 George sailed for New York on
the White Star liner *Olympic*. On the voyage he spent a considerable
amount of time closeted in his cabin, planning his narrative of the
1922 expedition. He also enjoyed the experience of sailing through
an Atlantic gale and in a letter home described 'the furious wind and
lightning, and torrents of wind and rain and great waves hitting the
ship with a terrific punch'. He arrived in New York on 17 January
to find that Keedick had not been able to arrange a very extensive
programme for him and that his first lecture was not for another ten
days. He was taken to the luxurious Waldorf-Astoria Hotel where he
met the press agent who was responsible for circulating information
about their distinguished visitors. As he told Ruth:

> The young man wanted me to say that the great mountaineers of the
> expedition were all men of scientific training, or that mental training had
> more to do with the matter than physique. Can you imagine anything more
> childish? But I expect that is just what Americans are – boyish.

He also gave Ruth his first impressions of New York:

New York itself often gives the impression of a splendid gesture against a background of emptiness. Each individual skyscraper is making its own gesture, rather than being part of a whole street; and as you see their immense silhouettes against the sky, they are all playing a part in a grotesque world of toy giants.

His room was on the twelfth floor and he joked to reporters that he was getting his training for Everest by rejecting the elevator and walking up to his room 'without oxygen tanks'.

Despite the extensive hospitality that he received, George was never very happy during this tour of America. Inevitably he had to spend much of his time alone and he keenly felt the separation from his family, confiding to Ruth: 'It is much more difficult to go without you in this country than ever it was in India.' He used his spare time writing his chapters for the 1922 expedition book and revising his lecture notes to suit an American audience. As he told Ruth:

> I've been busy [...] ever since I wrote, firstly finishing my chapters [...] and then with the lecture, much more work than you would suppose, cutting out one scrap and another, making a new beginning and a new end, incorporating Somervell's slides and about ten showing the reconnaissance, and most important of all, winnowing it all over to get the expression better for an American audience.

He gave his opening lecture in Washington on 26 January. Although he was disappointed at the reaction of the matinée audience, whom he described as the most unresponsive crowd I ever talked to – 'never a clap when I meant them to applaud and almost never a laugh', he was pleased with his performance in the evening:

> This evening it came right off, from the first word to the last. I did what I liked with them; they took all my points; it was technically better than any lecture I've ever given, either year, and had any amount of spontaneity, too. There: if it doesn't 'take' now – well, I can do no more.

He was given an enthusiastic reception in Philadelphia where more than 3,000 people attended his two lectures and he received good reviews in the local press. Well satisfied with his progress, he returned to New York, where he was due to give his first lecture at the Broadhurst theatre on 4 February. He knew that a good perform-ance and favourable press coverage there would ensure further lecture bookings.

In the meantime he was kept pleasantly occupied, dining with a cousin, dropping in at the University Club to read the weekly *Guardian*, and studying a collection of Boswell's letters in manuscript at the Morgan Library. After lunching with four doctors at their club, he went with them to the Presbyterian Hospital, where a thorough medical examination revealed that he had twice the normal lung capacity. He also attended a dinner of the American Alpine Club where he spoke about the problems of climbing Everest:

> There was not much fun or fizz in it, but it went well enough. After that, we sat on round the table while I was bombarded with questions. Altogether a very pleasant, homely party.

One lady he met on this occasion told him that she had 'climbed a peak in Alaska and endured a temperature of minus 60 degrees'. But she clearly did not impress him, for he later remarked that her intelligence appeared to have remained frozen ever since.

The New York lecture turned out to be a disappointing event. The theatre was only half full and the operator running the slides proved to be incompetent. Nonetheless the audience were appreciative:

> I had friends in the audience, amongst them all the members of the American Alpine Club who had been present at the dinner they gave me, so I didn't worry. I got them all right at the start; and they proved quite a pleasant and appreciative audience. They really went away fizzing, and I had reports of nice things said as they were going out.

But when he read the morning papers next day he was disappointed with their coverage. The Prohibition laws banning the sale of alcoholic drinks were still in force and the *New York Times* turned its coverage into anti-prohibition propaganda under the headline:

SAYS BRANDY AIDED MT. EVEREST PARTY – A Swig 27,000 Feet up 'Cheered Us All Up Wonderfully', Mallory Tells Audience.

But he was encouraged by the report in the *New York Tribune*, which appeared later in the day and praised him for his 'unaffected manner of speech which made him immediately a friend of his audience', and commented:

He described the perils of the climb in simple language, and kept his personal part in the expedition very much in the background.

From New York he went by train to Montréal, where he spoke to an appreciative audience. He enjoyed the hospitality of his Canadian host, Basil Williams, the Professor of history at McGill University, and especially the chance, under the tutelage of Basil's sixteen-year-old son John, of learning to ski in the Laurentian Hills. As he told Ruth:

I really began to learn something about it and had some glorious runs downhill. The clear days of a Canadian winter are very delightful, but it is cold.

On his return to New York, George learned that, despite his own highly praised performances, the lecture tour had not captured the public interest. The New York lecture had lost money and the one in Montréal had only made $48. Keedick reported to the Everest Committee that although Mallory was 'a fine fellow and gives a good lecture [...] the American public don't seem to be interested in the subject'. The financial failure of his American tour was very disappointing to Mallory as he had hoped that it would lead to financial stability for his family. He wrote to Ruth reporting the situation:

The lecture tour simply isn't coming off. [...] Don't be terribly disappointed. We shall be poorer than I hoped for a bit.

A few more lectures were arranged. He paid a second visit to Philadelphia where an audience of 1,200 heard him at the University Museum. At Boston he spoke to the Appalachian Mountain Club and was able to stay with Allston Burr, a Harvard graduate and member of the Alpine Club. And at Cambridge he spoke to a highly responsive audience, three-quarters of whom were Harvard undergraduates. The student newspaper, the *Harvard Crimson*, gave a full report of his lecture under the heading 'MALLORY THRILLS UNION AUDIENCE':

> Before an audience that filled the Living Room of the Union, Mr George Leigh Mallory described the attempt to ascend Mount Everest which took place last May. [...] Mr Mallory introduced his speech by asking 'What is the purpose of climbing Mount Everest?' He answered his question by saying in jest that it was of no use other than to fulfil the desire of the geologists for a stone from the summit and to show the physiologists at just what altitude human life becomes impossible.

George himself was pleased with his visit and reported to Ruth:

> They received me very well and were evidently thrilled and amused. There is no doubt that people over here are really impressed by the story and I shall feel that the lectures have been worthwhile even though the number remains small for the time spent in the country.

Finally, after a detour to Niagara Falls and a visit to his father's brother Wilfred in Toronto, he sailed for home on the *Saxonia*, which left New York on 31 March.

It was sometime during this American tour that, in response to a question why he wanted to climb Mount Everest, George gave his famous reply: 'Because it's there.' This answer appeared in a lengthy article in the *New York Times* of Sunday 18 March, which was probably based on an interview which George had given to an unnamed reporter soon after his arrival in New York. After being questioned about the scientific value of the expedition George agreed that there were valuable geological and botanical results, but said that

these were merely a by-product of mountaineering exploration. He
then went on to expand on his original answer:

> Everest is the highest mountain in the world, and no man has reached its
> summit. Its existence is a challenge. The answer is instinctive, a part, I suppose
> of man's desire to conquer the universe.

His feelings about the motivation for climbing Everest were also given
in the manuscript draft of a lecture in which he raised the question
whether the Mount Everest expedition served useful ends:

> The classic defence of the expedition made by Sir Francis Younghusband
> is simply this: he says by climbing Mount Everest you will stimulate the
> spirit of adventure throughout the English-speaking peoples of the world.
> Well, I can do no better than that. I hope what he says is true, and I must
> say I believe it is true.
>
>   But though Younghusband's words are a justification, they do not supply
> a motive. No one, I expect, would claim that he went to Mount Everest in
> order to stimulate the world. [...] No, I suppose we go to Mount Everest
> granted the opportunity, because – in a word – we can't help it. Or to state
> the matter rather differently, because we are mountaineers.

On his return to England George was delighted to find that the
problem of his future career might at last be resolved. On a recent train
journey from London to Cambridge Hinks had shared a compartment
with an old acquaintance, the Revd Dr David Cranage, the secretary of
the Board of Extra-mural Studies at Cambridge. It was expected that
in the aftermath of the war there would be an expansion of university
extension courses for working-class people and Cranage told Hinks
that he was looking for an assistant secretary to give lectures at local
centres around Cambridge as part of this work. Hinks immediately
suggested Mallory as a possible candidate for the post.

Delighted at the prospect, George sent Cranage a letter of
application on 20 April. He referred to his experience of teaching
working-class men in the army and said that he had: 'considerable
experience of public lecturing in Great Britain and in the USA in

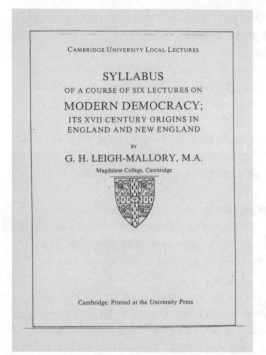

CAMBRIDGE UNIVERSITY LOCAL LECTURES

SYLLABUS
OF A COURSE OF SIX LECTURES ON
MODERN DEMOCRACY;
ITS XVII CENTURY ORIGINS IN
ENGLAND AND NEW ENGLAND

BY

G. H. LEIGH-MALLORY, M.A.
Magdalene College, Cambridge

Cambridge: Printed at the University Press

*The syllabus for George's
lectures at Hunstanton,
autumn 1923.*

connection with the two expeditions to Mount Everest'. He also sought the support of his friends. Arthur Benson, now Master of Magdalene College, Frank Fletcher, the headmaster of Charterhouse, Sir Francis Younghusband and the historian George Trevelyan all wrote letters in his support. Frank Fletcher praised George in glowing terms, referring to his 'singularly attractive personality, his enthusiasm for literature and great causes, his power of getting on with and winning the regard and friendship of all with whom he works'. And George Trevelyan thought that he would win many supporters for the adult education movement and added: 'He is one of the finest men whom the war has left us of that generation and his sane and steady idealism would be a great asset.'

There were twenty-five candidates and George was placed on a shortlist of five. Interviews were held on 8 May and he was appointed to the post. In a letter to Hinks he reported that:

There was a rather fierce battle in the end between me and another man with very strong academic qualifications and I rather thought I was going to be turned down. The fact that you had mentioned my name to Cranage before I applied was just one of the things that turned the scales in my favour. I'm very glad you put me on to the job.

He told Hinks that there was now no question of his doing any more lectures for the Everest Committee as he was required to start work more or less at once and added:

An even more serious matter is my poor diminished chance of going on the next expedition. I didn't at any point dare to bring up that question for fear of jeopardising my chances; and it will be difficult to bring it up now.

All George's friends were pleased at his success and Geoffrey Young wrote to congratulate him:

Few things could have given greater delight! May I claim a little selfish share in it? For – as you will probably not remember – when we were discussing Everest first, I said to Ruth, 'What George wants is a label, and this will give it.'

George was delighted with his new appointment, which he felt would offer him an interesting and fulfilling career. He moved at once to Cambridge, living in rented accommodation while he looked for a more permanent home. He threw himself into the work with great enthusiasm, helping with the organisation of the golden jubilee of Cambridge Local Lectures in July, and also assisting with the arrangement of the summer schools in the long vacation. In the autumn he started a course of lectures at Hunstanton on the seventeenth-century origins of modern democracy, and also gave tutorial classes in modern history at Raunds. At the end of October he moved his family into Herschel House, a large house in Herschel Road, Cambridge. He was to enjoy life there for just four months – because the question of Everest had broken out again.

FOURTEEN

PLANS FOR A THIRD EXPEDITION 1923-1924

Early in 1923 plans for another expedition to go to Everest in the following year were set in motion, and in April the Alpine Club appointed a committee to select the expedition members. George was invited to serve on this committee. General Charles Bruce was now the president of the Alpine Club and also chairman of the Mount Everest Committee, and it was unanimously agreed that he should be invited once again to lead the expedition. The first meeting of the selection committee was held on 1 May. In his notes of that meeting George recorded that it was clear that Norton and Somervell would go out again and that of new candidates Bentley Beetham and Noel Odell appeared the likeliest. After discussing other names he added the enigmatic reference 'Self?' At that stage the question of his involvement seemed very doubtful. He had just started a new job and he thought it most unlikely that the university would agree to let him go. But, on 18 October, Hinks wrote to Dr Cranage pressing for Mallory's inclusion in the party:

> The Mount Everest Committee are very anxious that Mallory should be a member of the expedition next year, and that everything possible should be done by them to assist him in obtaining leave from the University. [...] I can only ask you to convey to the proper quarters the assurance that Mallory's co-operation next year is of high importance in the opinion of the Mount Everest Committee to the success of their enterprise.

On 24 October the Cambridge Lecture Committee unanimously agreed to give Mallory six months leave at half-pay.

George now had to make the final decision for himself. Everest had already brought him fame and he was a married man with children. He had no need to risk everything again a third time on the mountain. But, after all his efforts on the two previous expeditions, he had a natural desire to be in at the finish. He knew that he was regarded as one of the finest mountaineers in the country and that it was expected that he would go out to Everest again. It was thought that his unrivalled experience of the first two expeditions would be of great assistance on the third attempt. As he wrote to his father:

> You'll see that most likely I shall be free to go, and it will therefore rest with me to make the choice. You may imagine that it isn't easy, and I look for guidance as to what is right. [...] My present feeling is that I have to look at it from the point of view of loyalty to the expedition and of carrying through a task begun.

Eventually, after discussing the matter fully with Ruth, he decided to go. He wrote again to his father:

> It's all settled, and I'm to go again. I only hope this is the right decision. It has been a fearful tug. I've had to think precisely what I was wanted for. They think I can help to keep it all safe; and I think that too a bit.

His father replied expressing his approval:

> Though of course your decision about Mount Everest must bring us an anxious time, still I feel you are right and congratulate you on having so decided. [...] Our thoughts and prayers will be with you all the time, and (needless to say) our very heartiest wishes for your success. It is most gratifying that the Everest committee appreciate all you have done so greatly and that the Cambridge Committee have risen so nobly to the occasion. [...] Ruth, too, is very good to give you up again. [...] We are wondering much if you will be able to come and see us before you go. Very much love, dear old man.

In view of some doubts over Bruce's continued good health, careful thought was given to the appointment of the climbing leader, who would act as Bruce's second-in-command and would take over if the General had to withdraw. After much deliberation Colonel Edward Norton, who had been such a success on the 1922 expedition, was appointed to this post in mid-October. General Bruce had a high opinion of Norton and in his report on the 1922 expedition members had written of him:

> The great success of the expedition. Is a first rate all round mountaineer, and full of every sort of interest.

It might have been thought that this post would have gone to Mallory in view of his unrivalled experience on Everest. But, at the time of the appointment, his participation in the expedition was not at all certain. Moreover, the duties of the climbing leader, who has responsibility for all activity on the mountain at Camp III and above, were to a large extent managerial. Even George's staunchest supporters could not claim that he had managerial skills. His absolute ambition to reach the summit was known to all, but it was also clear that his judgement was sometimes clouded by an impulsiveness and an impatience for action. It was felt that he would be more effective when there was some other leader to direct his great skills and to channel his restless energy and drive. In the event, General Bruce was taken ill on the approach march to Everest and Norton had to take over the leadership. His subsequent actions proved how right the committee had been. He showed himself to be a natural leader, never afraid to consult and always giving the credit to those whose ideas he adopted. He was respected by all members of the expedition and his authority was never questioned.

The other members of the climbing party were Howard Somervell, Geoffrey Bruce, Bentley Beetham, Noel Odell, Andrew Irvine and John de Vere Hazard. Howard Somervell had been one of the great successes of the 1922 expedition and General Bruce had written of him:

Stands by himself from the point of view of the Himalaya in his capacity as an absolute glutton for hard work, not so much that he is better on any particular day as for his extraordinary capacity for going day after day. He is a wonderful goer and climber.

He had had an outstanding season in the Alps in 1923, during which he had climbed more than thirty peaks in six weeks, and he was now working as a medical missionary in Travancore in south India. In addition to his fine surgical skills he was a gifted musician, who later composed the music to accompany John Noel's film of the expedition. He was also a talented artist and several of his paintings were chosen as illustrations for the 1924 expedition book. Geoffrey Bruce, who had also been highly praised for his contribution in 1922, was, in addition to his climbing duties, appointed to a wide-ranging post as adjutant. The general intended him to act as his right-hand man in the administration of the expedition.

Bentley Beetham, a schoolmaster from County Durham, was a renowned Lakeland mountaineer who also had a distinguished record in the Alps. He had been Somervell's climbing companion during his remarkable 1923 season. Noel Odell was an experienced Alpinist who had served with the Royal Engineers in the war and was now working in the Persian oilfields as a geologist and mining engineer. He had accompanied the 1921 and 1923 Oxford University expeditions to the Norwegian Arctic island of Spitsbergen as a geologist, and he was widely respected in the mountaineering world. In addition to his climbing duties he was asked to act as the expedition's oxygen officer and in June 1923 he spent a couple of days testing the proposed equipment in North Wales.

Andrew Irvine, at twenty-one, was by far the youngest member of the party. He came from Birkenhead and was an undergraduate in his third year reading chemistry at Merton College, Oxford. He had rowed in the Oxford boat in 1922, which lost to Cambridge by four and a half lengths, and again in 1923, when Oxford won a famous victory, their first for ten years, by three-quarters of a length. In the summer of 1923 he had been invited to join the second Oxford University expedition to Spitsbergen where he had been a member of the

sledging party and had come to the notice of Noel Odell, the
expedition geologist. Odell had been very impressed by his stamina
and enterprise in difficult circumstances, and by his good humour
and unselfishness. He had also noted that Irvine was something of a
mechanical genius, who had made several useful suggestions to him
for dealing with the problems encountered by the proposed Everest
oxygen equipment.

On returning to England, Odell had strongly recommended Irvine
for inclusion in the 1924 Everest team. Irvine's climbing experience
was limited to British mountains and, after receiving the Everest
Committee's invitation, he spent three weeks at Christmas and New
Year at Mürren in Switzerland under the guidance of Arnold Lunn.
His inclusion in the Everest party was something of an experiment
and, in a comment on his selection, George told Geoffrey Young:
'Irvine represents our attempt to get one superman though lack of
experience is against him'. Because of his outstanding practical skills
he was given the role of equipment officer.

John de Vere Hazard was an experienced Alpine climber. He was
selected on the recommendation of Major Henry Morshead, the
surveyor on the first two expeditions, who had served with him in
India and also on the Somme. Richard Graham, a schoolmaster from
Reading and a distinguished Lakeland climber and alpinist, was originally selected ahead of Hazard. But it then emerged that, as a Quaker,
he had been a conscientious objector and had remained at his teaching
post throughout the war. It seems that a member of the team protested
against his inclusion and when this news reached the press Graham
withdrew from the expedition. Both Mallory and Somervell leapt to
his defence and expressed their shame and anger at what had been
done. Somervell cabled from India his resignation from the Alpine
Club saying:

> I cannot conceive how the propriety of the Alpine Club could stomach
> such a low down trick after they had elected him in the full knowledge of
> his convictions. [...] It is a dirty piece of work.

George protested his outrage in a letter to General Bruce:

The sooner members of the party who feel such things learn to control their feelings and make the best of the party as they find it the better it will be for all of us. [...] I should have thought that a man who seemed to be good enough for yourself, Younghusband, Ronaldshay and Collie [...] may be good enough for any member of the party. And I further think that to ask a man to resign after he has been asked to join the expedition and the fact has been published in the press is simply a thing which is not done. [...] I have the strongest opposition to any member of the party who is agitating to turn down Graham after the invitation has been sent; and I hereby agitate against *him*. [...] Precious few men are so valuable that I would want to keep them in if they are determined to kick out Graham at this stage.

The records giving the details of this matter are not to be found in the Royal Geographical Society archives and it is not clear which member of the team had caused this upset. In the event Somervell's resignation from the Alpine Club did not take place.

Captain John Noel once again accompanied the expedition with the aim of making a film of every aspect of its progress. He agreed with the Everest Committee that he should be responsible for his own expenses and also pay £8,000 for the full photographic rights. Edward Shebbeare of the Indian Forest Service was appointed the official transport officer and was to join the party in Darjeeling. The team was completed by the appointment of Richard Higston as medical officer and official naturalist. He had been on the 1913 Indo-Russian survey expedition and was now an RAF surgeon in Mesopotamia. He would travel from his post at Baghdad to join the party in India.

Once George had taken the decision to go, he felt a load off his mind. He threw himself into his busy round of lectures and secretarial duties, and also devoted as much time as he could to settling in to their new home in Cambridge. He took delight in all the practical things which had to be done: choosing wall paper and curtains for the dining-room, painting the drawing-room, and fitting a wire fence around the tennis court. After spending Christmas at Westbrook, he took Ruth to the Peak District for a short climbing holiday in the new year. On 13 February he signed an agreement with the Mount Everest Committee, one paragraph of which read:

I agree that I shall join the Expedition at my own risk as to the consequences
and the Committee shall not be responsible for any damage, personal or
otherwise, which I or any dependent, may suffer during the continuance of
the Expedition or on my journey to, or back from, Darjeeling.

George was well aware of the risk he was running. When a member
of the audience at a lecture at Taunton said how thrilled he must be
to be going out again, he replied: 'You know, I am leaving my wife
and young children behind me.' And he confided to his Cambridge
friend Geoffrey Keynes: 'This is going to be more like war than
mountaineering. I don't expect to come back.'

Before the expedition set sail, George took Ruth to stay with his
parents at Birkenhead. Also in Birkenhead lived the family of Andrew
Irvine. On 28 February the Liverpool Wayfarers Club give a dinner
for the four expedition members who were sailing from Liverpool:
Mallory, Irvine, Beetham and Hazard. The fathers of Mallory and
Irvine were invited as guests. The party sailed next day on the SS
California. There was a westerly gale blowing and the two tugs had
difficulty in pulling the liner away from the quayside. In his first letter
to Ruth from the ship George wrote:

I am glad you decided to abandon waving. We weren't off till 8.30 or
thereabouts as the two tugs provided were hopelessly beaten by the wind.
It was a wild night, that first one; and yesterday in the bay was wild too,
with wind and rain a plenty scudding across the waste steel-grey white
capped waters.

Once again George enjoyed the companionship of his fellow expedition members on the voyage. He shared a cabin with Beetham,
whom he considered 'good-humoured and unselfish' and a table in
the dining room with Irvine, whom he described as 'one to depend
on for everything except perhaps conversation'. Determined to be
fit, he took regular exercise in the gymnasium and occasionally ran
ten times round the deck. He was persuaded to enter a potato race
and triumphantly reported: 'I had a brilliant success and was only
knocked out in the final, where one potato was really impossible.'

As always he spent much of his time reading, and he also started to learn Hindi.

It is clear from letters which George wrote on the voyage that he was constantly wrestling with their plans for the summit and that he was now seriously considering the use of oxygen. To his sister Mary he wrote:

> Irvine is a great dab at things mechanical and has some criticisms to make; and there are certainly a good many chances that it will go wrong or break if we use it. [...] However, I rather expect we shall use it, as we can carry 50 per cent more oxygen than last year with the same weight. Norton was keen to go up without oxygen from 26,000 but we've got to camp higher than that to have a chance. Anyway, we've got to get up this time; and if we wait for it and make full preparations, instead of dashing up at the first moment, some of us will reach the summit, I believe. [...] I wish Irvine had had a season in the Alps.

And he told Tom Longstaff:

> I'm dead against trying without oxygen from 26,000 – we should simply knock out 3 or 4 of the best and be jolly lucky if they had the sense to turn back in time... And I'm dead against making ill-prepared dashes; it's got to be all or nothing this time; we don't want to break any more records for height unless we reach the summit; and the only way is to start as high as possible. Personally, if I were to be one of a sans-oxygen party I should like to sleep 3 nights at CP IV and 2 at CP V; leave Camp V by moonlight to establish VI; use oxygen at night, partly in a closed tent so to get the benefit of the CO_2 at both V and VI.

This letter is significant for showing his realisation of the need for an early start from their high camps. As George's son John points out in his foreword, one of the main advantages which modern expeditions have is that the use of a head lamp enables them to leave camp several hours before dawn.

After landing at Bombay the four climbers travelled to Darjeeling where on 21 March they met the other members of the expedition.

They were the last to arrive and had just five days to make final preparations for their departure. After a consultation with Norton, George
arranged with his sister Mary, now living in Colombo, for regular
weather reports to be sent. He was very pleased with the arrangements
Norton was making and wrote to Ruth:

> Norton has got the whole organisation under his hand. [...] All the stores
> for the high camps have practically been settled already. He is going to be
> an ideal second to Bruce.

All members of the expedition left Darjeeling together on 26 March.
At Kalimpong they separated into two parties, and George travelled
in the second with Norton, Odell, Hingston, Irvine and Shebbeare.
Apart from a few twinges from his old ankle injury he felt in fine
shape and wrote to Ruth:

> I must tell you, dearest one, how wonderfully fit I have been these last days,
> much better at this stage, I'm sure, than either in '21 or '22. I feel full of energy
> and strength, and walk uphill here already almost as in the Alps.

Unfortunately, worries now emerged over General Bruce's health. It
was only with extreme reluctance that the two doctors who examined
him in London had agreed to him going on the expedition. For some
days he had not been feeling well and it was decided, that accompanied by
Hingston, the medical officer, he should to to Kampa Dzong by a lower
route than that taken by the rest of the party. As George told Ruth:

> The General's trouble has been an irregular pulse, and he and Hingston are
> both nervous about the effects of these altitudes on his heart. Consequently
> he is not coming with us to Kampa Dzong [...] but by another way which
> will allow him to camp lower.

On 7 April Bruce celebrated his fifty-eighth birthday with a bottle of
rum which had been specially sent out from England by his brother,
but two days later he collapsed from a severe attack of malaria.
Hingston insisted on accompanying him back to India and stipulated

that he should withdraw from the expedition. Norton took over the leadership and immediately appointed Mallory as his deputy and leader of the climbing party. George told Ruth:

> Norton takes command; and we couldn't have a better commander. He will do it much better than I could have done had I been in his place, if only because he can talk the lingoes freely. He has appointed me second-in-command in his place, and also leader of the climbers altogether. I'm bound to say I feel some little satisfaction in the latter position.

Mallory and Norton worked well together and held regular discussions over the best way to make their attempt on the summit. It was Mallory who devised the final plan. There were to be three camps above the North Col: Camp V at 25,500ft, Camp VI at 26,500ft and Camp VII at 27,200ft. There would be two summit attempts, each of two men, one party equipped with oxygen and one without. The oxygen party would try for the summit from Camp VI, while the other pair would make their attempt the same day from Camp VII. Both groups would act independently but would be able to support each other if the need arose. George outlined these plans in a letter to Longstaff on 19 April, which again showed his realisation of the need for an early start:

> The two parties start an hour or more before daylight, in full moonlight and windless air, we hope, and meet on the summit.

He also expressed his appreciation of Irvine's work on the oxygen apparatus:

> Irvine is a mechanical genius and has chopped up the O_2 apparatus, cutting out half the leaky taps & reducing the weight by 3lbs and making the whole much more portable in view of rocks to climb or steps to cut; and he's one of the best.

Norton announced the composition of the two climbing parties after dinner on 21 April. Somervell and Norton were to climb without

oxygen, and the oxygen party was to consist of Mallory and Irvine.
That night Irvine commented in his diary:

> I'm awfully glad that I'm with Mallory in the first lot. But I wish ever so
> much that it was a non-oxygen attempt.

Three days later George wrote to Ruth explaining the reasons
behind the choice of climbers:

> The question as to which of the first two parties should be led by Somervell
> and which by me was decided on two grounds. (1) On the assumption that
> the oxygen party would be less exhausted and be in the position of helping
> the other, it seemed best that I should use oxygen and help with the descent.
> (2) It seemed more likely on his last year's performance that Somervell would
> recover after a gasless attempt to be useful again later.
>
> It was obvious that either Irvine or Odell should come with me in the first
> gas party. Odell is in charge of the gas, but Irvine has been the engineer at
> work on the apparatus. What was provided was full of leaks and faults; and he
> has practically invented a new instrument, using up only a few of the old parts
> and cutting out much that was useless and likely to cause trouble. Moreover,
> the remaining parties had to be considered; it wouldn't do to make Irvine
> the partner of Geoffrey Bruce, as they lack mountaineering experience. And
> so Irvine will come with me. He will be an extraordinarily stout companion,
> very capable with the gas and with cooking apparatus. The only doubt is to
> what extent his lack of mountaineering experience will be a handicap. I hope
> the ground will be sufficiently easy.

And in a confident mood, he continued:

> Only four marches, starting tomorrow morning, to the Rongbuk monas-
> tery! We're getting very near now. On May 3rd four of us will leave the
> Base Camp and begin the upward trek, and on May 17th or thereabouts
> we should reach the summit. [...] The telegram announcing our success,
> if we succeed, will precede this letter, I suppose; but it will mention no
> names. How you will hope that I was one of the conquerors! And I don't
> think you'll be disappointed.

FIFTEEN

THE LAST ADVENTURE 1924

The expedition celebrated its arrival at Base Camp on 29 April with a five-course dinner complete with champagne. With a stronger party than in 1922 and with carefully laid plans for their attempt on the summit, they were optimistic over their chances of success. But unfortunately in the days that followed, a prolonged spell of very bad weather ruined their plans. Camps I and II were quickly reoccupied, and on 5 May Mallory, Irvine, Odell and Hazard set out from Camp II with the intention of re-establishing Camps III and IV.

But during the following week fresh snow and strong winds prevented them from getting more than a few loads to Camp III, and efforts to establish it in any permanent manner taxed the strength of the climbers to the utmost limit. The morale of the porters also became very low, and two died after being brought down the mountain in a very poor condition, one from a cerebral haemorrhage and the other from severe frostbite in the legs. At last, after many heroic efforts in blizzard conditions, Norton took the decision on 11 May 'to evacuate III for the present and retire all ranks to Base Camp'.

Despite all these setbacks George tried to maintain his intellectual interests. In a letter to Ruth he described an evening spent at Camp III on 9 May during this trying time:

> I produced *The Spirit of Man* and began reading one thing and another. [...] We all agreed that 'Kubla Khan' was a good sort of poem. Irvine was

rather poetry-shy, but seemed to be favourably impressed by the Epitaph to Gray's 'Elegy'. Odell was much inclined to be interested and liked the last lines of 'Prometheus Unbound'. S [Somervell] who knows quite a lot of English literature, had never read a poem of Emily Brontë's and was happily introduced.

Irvine's diary for this period gives a clear picture of the difficult conditions they were facing, and puts George's apparently serene attitude into perspective. On the same day that George was writing his letter, Irvine recorded:

Perfectly bloody day – nothing else will describe it. Wind and driven snow. [...] Somervell and Odell decided that it was too filthy weather to attempt the North Col. [...] Has snowed hard all afternoon.

And on 10 May he noted:

Had a terrible night with wind and snow. I don't know how the tent stood it. Very little sleep and about 2in of snow over everything in the tent.

But it is clear that George was bitterly disappointed at their failure to make progress. He told Ruth: 'It has been a very trying time with everything against us.' And, reflecting on their exhausting experiences at Camp III, Somervell later commented:

It was largely this first week at No.3 camp that reduced our strength and made us – by the time when we finally climbed as far as we could, three weeks later – thin and weak and almost invalided, instead of being fit and strong as we had been during the 1922 ascent.

At base camp John Noel, the expedition photographer, invited George to share his large photographic tent and later commented:

I had opportunities of observing his restless energy and ambition. He seemed ill at ease; always scheming and planning. It was obvious to me he felt this set-back more acutely than any of us.

George himself thought that he had great strength left and, as he told Ruth, he considered that his summit partner, Irvine, had a resolute attitude:

> Irvine [...] has been wonderfully hard-working and brilliantly skilful about the oxygen. Against him is his youth (though it is very much for him, some ways) – hard things seem to hit him a bit harder – and his lack of mountaineering training and practice, which must tell to some event when it comes to climbing rocks or even to saving energy on the easiest ground. However, he'll be an ideal companion, and with as stout a heart as you could wish to find. If each of us keeps his strength as it is at present, we should go well together. [...] Perhaps we shall go to the top on Ascension Day, May 29th.

And he told his mother:

> Irvine is the star of the new members. He is a very fine fellow, has been doing excellently up to date, and should prove a splendid companion on the mountain. I should think the *Birkenhead News* – is it? – ought to have something to say if he and I reach the top together.

It is clear that in preparation for their summit bid Mallory and Irvine were forming a closer relationship. Irvine's diary, which normally referred to all expedition members by their surnames, now contains frequent references to 'George'.

The expedition stayed at Base Camp for six nights, and on 15 May Norton took all members down to the Rongbuk monastery to receive the blessing of the Lama. The campaign began again on 17 May, and three days later Mallory, Norton and Odell made a route from Camp III to the North Col, where they established Camp IV. In order to avoid the steep slope swept by the avalanche in 1922, George had at one stage to lead 200ft up an ice wall and a narrow chimney. Norton later commented:

> Confronted with a formidable climbing obstacle, Mallory's behaviour was always characteristic: you could positively see his nerves tighten up like fiddle strings. Metephorically speaking he girt up his loins, and his first

instinct was to jump into the lead. Up the wall and chimney he led here, climbing carefully, neatly, and in that beautiful style that was all his own.

They were exhausted by the effort of this climb and their return to Camp III was a hazardous affair. First Norton and then one of the porters slipped on the ice, and later George, who was leading and unroped, fell into a crevasse. He described to Ruth what happened:

> I went in with snow tumbling all around me, down luckily only about ten feet before I fetched up half-blind and breathless to find myself most precariously supported only by my ice-axe somehow caught across the crevasse and still held in my right hand – and below was a very unpleasant black hole. I had some nasty moments before I got comfortably wedged and began to yell for help up through the round hole I had come through. [...] However I soon got tired of shouting – they hadn't seen me from above – and bringing the snow down a little at a time, I made a hole out towards the side (the crevasse ran down a slope) [...] and so extricated myself.

The weather now deteriorated again and Hazard and twelve porters who had carried loads up to Camp IV were stranded there for two days. On 23 May, taking advantage of a break in the weather, Hazard decided to come down. He arrived at Camp III at 5 p.m., but was accompanied by only eight of the porters. Norton described what had happened:

> It appeared that he had gone first across the traverse to test the condition of the fresh snow, which rendered it a very dangerous passage; eight men had followed him, one crossing at a time, but the last four had turned back.

The situation was now very serious and emergency plans were made for a rescue. Snow fell for much of the night and both Mallory and Somervell had sore throats and bad coughs, but next day, accompanied by Norton, they set out for Camp IV. In some places they had to make their way through snow which was waist-deep. When they reached the steep slope under the shelf on which Camp IV was placed, Somervell led on a diagonal traverse, while Mallory and Norton safeguarded him on an ice-axe belay. Ten yards short of the shelf on which the four porters were sitting, Somervell came to the end of the rope. Norton called to the porters and told them to make their own way down one by one very carefully to join Somervell. The first two climbed down safely and were passed back on a tight rope. The second two made the mistake of starting together and the snow gave way under them. At first it seemed inevitable that they would shoot into space over the edge of the cliff, but suddenly they came to a stop as the snow under their feet bound itself to the slope. Norton described Somervell's final solution:

> Somervell then untied the rope from his waist, drove his ice axe in up to its head in the soft snow, passed the rope round it and strained it so as to make every foot he could, while Mallory and I held our end at extreme arm's length. Holding his own in the same way he then let himself down to the extreme length of the rope and of his own arm, while with the other hand he grasped, one after the other, the two porters by the scruff of the neck and pulled them back to the anchor of his axe.

The rescue party set out to return to Camp III and were soon overtaken by darkness. Before reaching the camp they were met by Odell and Noel, who had set out carrying hot soup in thermos flasks. Noel later described the scene:

> We carried lanterns and made our way laboriously through the snow in the footsteps which the men had made that morning. We had toiled through the darkness for about one and half hours when, in reply to our frequent calls, we heard answering shouts. They had seen the welcoming twinkle of our lanterns. When we met, the whole lot of them sank down in the snow. they were absolutely done! The porters were like drunken men, not knowing what was happening. Norton, Somervell and Mallory hardly spoke.

The rescue had succeeded, but at a very serious cost to their precious reserves of strength. All members of the expedition now withdrew to Camp I. George wrote to Ruth expressing his feelings:

> Dear Girl, this has been a bad time altogether. I look back on tremendous
> efforts and exhaustion and dismal looking out of a tent door onto a world
> of snow and vanishing hopes.

Noel noted that George looked ill and spent much of his time in his
sleeping bag. In his opinion George's strength had been sapped, and it
was only his nervous energy which was keeping him going.

Plans were now made for a third phase of the campaign. In order
to reduce the number of porters required in support, the decision
was taken to send two summit parties without oxygen: George was to
make the first attempt with Geoffrey Bruce as his partner. At Norton's
request George wrote part of the dispatch to *The Times* revealing the
grim determination underlying this last attempt:

> The issue will shortly be decided. The third time we walk up the East
> Rongbuk Glacier will be the last, for better or worse. We have counted our
> wounded and know, roughly, how much to strike off the strength of our
> little army as we plan the next act of battle.

Before leaving, George wrote a last letter to Ruth:

> Darling, I wish you the best I can – that your anxiety will be at an end
> before you get this, with the best news, which will also be the quickest.
> It is fifty to one against us, but we'll have a whack yet and do ourselves
> proud. Great love to you.

And to David Pye he expressed his misgivings:

> We are on the point of moving up again, and the adventure appears more
> desperate than ever. [...] All sound plans are now abandoned for two
> consecutive dashes without gas.

Mallory and Bruce arrived at Camp IV on 31 May and the next day,
despite a fierce wind from the north-west, they established Camp V at
25,500 feet. They planned to site Camp VI at 27,000 feet and then go
for the summit on 2 June. But next morning only one of the porters

was fit to continue, and they had no option but to abandon the attempt. Their places were taken by the second party of Norton and Somervell, who established Camp VI at 26,800 feet on 3 June. They made their summit bid on the next day. They chose a route about 500ft below the north-east ridge climbing diagonally along a bad of yellow sandstone. They made very slow progress. As Norton later reported:

> Our pace was wretched. My ambition was to do twenty consecutive paces uphill without a pause, to rest and pant elbow on bent knee; yet I never remember achieving it – thirteen was nearer the mark. [...] Every five or ten minutes we had to sit down for a minute or two, and we must have looked a sorry couple.

At 28,000ft Somervell, who was plagued by a racking cough, decided that he could go no further. He found a suitable ledge where he could sit in the sun and urged Norton to go on alone. Norton, although he was now beginning to see double, continued over steep slabs and treacherous snow for about an hour and reached a height reckoned to be 28,126ft, less than a thousand feet below the summit, before he too knew that he must turn back. As he descended towards Somervell he asked him to come up with a rope as he was beginning to suffer from snowblindness. Together the two made their slow way down. They had not gone far before Somervell's ice-axe slipped from his grip and plunged down the mountain. As they passed through Camp IV Somervell picked up a tent-pole as a substitute for his axe. The going was easier now and they unroped, an action which nearly proved Somervell's undoing. As he later wrote:

> Somewhere about 25,000ft high, when darkness was gathering, I had one of my fits of coughing and dislodged something in my throat which stuck so that I could breathe neither in nor out. I could not, of course, make a sign to Norton, or stop him, for the rope was off now; so I sat in the snow to die whilst he walked on, little knowing that his companion was awaiting the end only a few yards behind him. I made one or two attempts to breathe, but nothing happened. Finally, I pressed my chest with both hands, gave one last almighty push – and the obstruction came up. What a relief! Coughing

up a little blood, I once more breathed really freely – more freely than I had done for some days. Though the pain was intense, yet I was a new man, and was soon going down at a better pace than ever to rejoin Norton.

Mallory and Odell met them above the North Col and escorted them down to Camp IV where Irvine was brewing tea and soup.

That day Mallory had gone down to Camp III. Finding some of the porters to be still fit for action, he had returned with them to Camp IV and he now told Norton that he had decided to make one more attempt on the summit, this time with oxygen, taking Irvine as his companion. Norton, who was now completely snow-blind, was full of admiration for Mallory's energy and strength of will, but regretted that he had chosen Irvine rather than Odell. Odell was immeasurably more experienced as a mountaineer and, after being very slow to acclimatise, was now going very well. Mallory said that he preferred Irvine because of his peculiar talent in dealing with the oxygen apparatus.

Mallory and Irvine spent 5 June making preparations for this final attempt. Odell was to provide support, climbing to Camps V and VI a day behind the summit party. Irvine, who was suffering badly from sunburn, made the final entry in his diary:

> My face is perfect agony. Have prepared two oxygen apparatus for our start tomorrow morning.

Next day Mallory and Irvine with eight porters set out from Camp IV at 8.40 a.m. Odell captured the moment of their departure with a photograph. They made good progress and, after sending down four of their porters, spent the night at Camp V. On 7 June they arrived at Camp VI. That night Mallory sent down the remaining four porters, with two notes written in pencil on a scrap of paper torn out of a notebook. The first was to Odell:

> We're awfully sorry to have left things in such a mess – our Unna Cooker rolled down the slope at the last moment. Be sure of getting back to IV tomorrow in time to evacuate before dark as I hope to. In the tent I must have left a compass – for the Lord's sake rescue it: we are without. To here

on 90 atmospheres for the two days – so we'll probably go on two cylinders – but it's a bloody load for climbing. Perfect weather for the job!

The other note was for John Noel, who would be looking for photographs:

We'll probably start early tomorrow (8th) in order to have clear weather. It won't be too early to start looking out for us either crossing the rock band under the pyramid or going up skyline at 8 p.m. [Mallory obviously meant a.m.].

The porters reported that the two climbers had been 'going exceedingly strong with oxygen'.

Odell received Mallory's message shortly after arriving at Camp V. The next morning he set out alone for Camp VI. At first it was a clear morning and not especially cold, but later clouds began to form and there was intermittent snow. Just after midday, when he had reached about 26,000 feet, there was a sudden clearing in the cloud. Odell later described for *The Times* what he saw:

At 12.50, just after I had emerged from a state of jubilation at finding the first definite fossils on Everest, there was a sudden clearing of the atmosphere, and the entire summit ridge and final peak of Everest were unveiled. My eyes became fixed on one tiny black spot silhouetted on a small snow-crest beneath a rock-step in the ridge; the black spot moved. Another black spot became apparent and moved up the snow to join the other on the crest. The first then approached the great rock-step and shortly emerged at the top; the second did likewise. Then the whole fascinating vision vanished, enveloped in cloud once more.

Convinced that he had caught a glimpse of Mallory and Irvine, hours behind their schedule but 'going strong for the top', Odell continued to Camp VI. As he arrived the weather deteriorated and a blizzard raged across the north face. After sheltering in the tent for a while, it occurred to him that the weather might have driven the climbers to return. Since visibility was down to a few yards, they would have difficulty in finding the tent, so he climbed 200ft above the camp, whistling and yodelling as he went. There was no answering call and, after sheltering behind a rock for a while, he returned to the tent. After two hours the blizzard ended and the north face was bathed in sunshine – but of the two climbers there was no trace. Remembering the instruction to be back at Camp IV in time to evacuate that night, Odell left Mallory's compass on the floor of the tent and descended to the North Col where he was joined by Hazard. It was a clear evening and after having some warm soup they turned out to wait for the climbers' return. the face of Everest was floodlit by the light of the moon reflected from the glacier, but as the night wore on there was no sign of the returning climbers.

Next morning they scanned the upper camps through their field-glasses but could see no signs of movement. At noon Odell decided to climb back up the mountain. He took two Sherpas with him to Camp V where he spent the night, and next morning he continued alone. On reaching Camp VI one glance inside the tent told him the worst. Nothing had been touched since his last visit, and Mallory's compass still lay where he had left it. Although there could now be no doubt of Mallory and Irvine's fate, Odell set off to follow their most likely line of ascent. He struggled upwards for two hours until at last, with a feeling of utter despair, he slowly came to a halt. As he later commented:

> This upper part of Everest must be indeed the remotest and least hospitable spot on earth, but at no time more emphatically and impressively so than when a darkened atmosphere hides its features and a gale races over its cruel face. And how and when more cruel could it ever seem than when baulking one's every step to find one's friends.

Reluctantly he made his way back to Camp VI, and dragging the two sleeping bags from the tent he hauled them up to a patch of snow and placed them in the form of a letter 'T'. Down at Camp V the wait-ing Hazard knew what that meant – 'No Trace' – and he immediately passed the message down to Camp III where Norton had been waiting in suspense for the past four days. As Norton later commented:

The memory of those days is such that Camp III must remain to all of us the most hateful place in the world.

After retrieving Mallory's compass, Odell prepared to descend the mountain. He later recorded his feelings on leaving Camp VI for the last time.

Closing up the tent and leaving its other contents as my friends had left them, I glanced up at the mighty summit above me, which ever and anon deigned to reveal its cloud-wreathed features. It seemed to look down with cold indifference on me, mere puny man, and howl derision in wind-gusts at my petition to yield up its secret – this mystery of my friends.

On receiving the news that no trace had been found of Mallory and Irvine, Norton immediately dispatched a coded telegram to be sent to London. No further attempts were made to search for the missing climbers and by 12 June all members of the expedition were back in Base Camp. As Norton wrote:

We were a sad little party; from the first we accepted the loss of our comrades in that rational spirit which all of our generation had learnt in the Great War, and there was never a tendency to a morbid harping on the irrevocable. But the tragedy was very near; our friends' vacant tents and vacant places at table were a constant reminder to us of what the atmosphere of the camp would have been had things gone differently.

Three days were spent in packing up, during which a cairn was built to commemorate the twelve men who had died on the three Everest expeditions: Dr Kellas, nine Sherpas, and now George Mallory and Sandy Irvine. On 14 June the expedition set out for home. The news reached London on 19 June and after Ruth Mallory had been given the news she went for a long walk with close friends.

On 17 October a memorial service for the two climbers was held in St Paul's Cathedral, at which the sermon was given by the Rt Revd Henry Paget, Bishop of Chester, from whose diocese both Mallory and Irvine had come. That evening there was a joint meeting of the

Alpine Club and the Royal Geographical Society in the Royal Albert Hall, at which Norton said of Mallory:

> A fire burnt in him, and it made him one of the two most formidable antagonists Everest has ever had. He was absolutely determined to conquer the mountain, and no one knows better than I do how for several months this year he devoted his whole mind and will to this object.
>
> At the same time those who suggest that he may have taken chances to achieve success in his last climb misrepresent him. For equally strong as his will to conquer was his sense of responsibility as leader of a party, and I know that he was prepared – nay, determined – to turn back however near the summit if it could not be reached in time to return to safety.

Many of George's friends wrote to Ruth expressing their deep sense of sorrow and loss. Robert Graves said of him:

> George was my first real friend, and he always remained so. [...] My only consolation at the moment is that he once told me on Snowdon that he hoped he'd die like that, climbing. [...] So like George to choose the highest and most dangerous mountain in the world.

His old climbing friend Cottie Sanders (now Mrs O'Malley) wrote:

> He was always taking one on further, showing one new roads and a fresh point of view. You know how he did that to people, better than anyone. He was so sound, so clear; he had such an extraordinarily delicate perception for all those things that he shaped one's own views without one's knowing it.

But perhaps the final word is best left to Ruth Mallory, writing to Geoffrey Young, whom she and George had found such a staunch friend throughout their married life:

> I know George did not mean to be killed; he meant not to be so hard that I did not a bit think he would be. [...] I don't think I do feel that his death makes me the least more proud of him. It is his life that I loved and love. I know absolutely that he could not have failed in courage or self-sacrifice.

Whether he got to the top of the mountain or did not [...] makes no difference to my admiration of him. I think I have got the pain separate. There
is so much of it, and it will go on for so long, that I must do that. [...]

Oh Geoffrey, if only it hadn't happened! It so easily might not have.

SIXTEEN

THIS MYSTERY
OF MY FRIENDS

'Mallory and Irvine may possibly have reached the summit; but they have not lived to tell us.' So wrote Sir Francis Younghusband at the start of his introduction to the 1924 expedition book. His words sum up the mystery which has remained unsolved ever since, and that last tantalising glimpse of the climbers high up on the north-east ridge, 'going strong for the top', has remained etched on the memory for the last eighty years.

Before leaving the mountain, Norton called a conference of expedition members to discuss what might have happened. With the single exception of Odell, they agreed that the most likely reason for the disaster was a slip by one of the climbers, possibly caused by the thick covering of fresh snow on the sloping slabs. Against this Odell argued that, if Mallory and Irvine had been successful, they could not have reached the summit before 3 p.m. at the earliest, five or six hours behind the schedule that Mallory had outlined in his note to John Noel. With only four hours of daylight left, it would have been almost impossible for them to have got back to Camp VI before nightfall, and they would most likely have been benighted on the mountain. But it was a fine night, and the absence of any light on the mountain after dark was, in Norton's view, conclusive against this theory:

> If the pair were benighted on the mountain, why was their torch [...] not visible to the eyes of those of us who watched for them so anxiously from

Camps IV and III? For a watch was kept on the mountain until long after dark from both camps; the night was clear, and from both probably, certainly from Camp IV, a light moving on the mountain must have been detected after dark. We had even arranged a signal – the letters S.O.S. in Morse code – which was to be sent repeatedly to Camp IV by any climbers benighted high on the mountain and unable to reach Camp IV.

Odell did not accept this argument:

To me it is by no means conclusive since anything might have happened, in the way of damage or loss of their lantern or flash-light, to have prevented their showing a light. And the same applies to the magnesium flares which we supposed that they carried. In the tent at Camp VI I found one of the latter, which indicates the possibility of their having forgotten them the morning of their departure.

When members of the 1933 expedition came upon the site of Camp VI, they found a torch still in working order in the remains of the tent. It is possible, therefore, that neither a torch nor any flares were taken on that final climb. Mallory had the reputation for being extremely absent-minded. On the 1922 expedition the transport officer, John Morris, recalled that on the approach march Mallory left things scattered about on the floor of his tent to such an extent that 'after the first few days we took it in turns to see that none of his kit was left behind'. And when members were being considered for the 1924 expedition General Bruce observed of him: 'He is a great dear, but forgets his boots on all occasions.'

There was the further question of whether Mallory would have continued the ascent to the summit knowing that this action would endanger his own life and that of his companion. He had always taken a responsible attitude towards climbing, and Norton felt that there was no doubt that he would have turned back if he felt that safety was at risk. But it must be remembered that this was his last chance of achieving his life's ambition, and Odell considered that the realisation that the summit was within his reach may have been too strong for him:

I know that Mallory had stated he would take no risks in any attempt on the final peak; but in action the desire to overcome, the craving for the victory that had become for him, as Norton has put it, an obsession, may have been too strong for him. The knowledge of his own proved powers of endurance, and those of his companion, may have urged him to make a bold bid for the summit. Irvine I know was willing, nay, determined, to expend his last ounce of energy, to 'go all out' as he put it, in an utmost effort to reach the top: for had not his whole training in another hardy pursuit been to inculcate the faculty of supreme final effort? And who of us that has wrestled with some Alpine giant in the teeth of a gale, or in a race with the darkness, would hold back when such a victory, such a triumph of human endeavour, was within our grasp?

Geoffrey Young took the same view:

After nearly 20 years' knowledge of Mallory as a mountaineer, I can say [...] that difficult as it would have been for any mountaineer to turn back with the only difficulty past – to Mallory it would have been an impossibility.

And John Noel, who had spent that fateful day at Camp IV anxiously waiting for a sighting, also expressed the same sentiments:

You can imagine how they must have been urged on by one dominating desire – the Summit. You can imagine how Mallory's energy of nerve, brain and muscle must have risen to the supreme effort of his life. You can imagine his spirit straining his physical strength to the last limits. The goal was in their grasp. Should they turn back and lose it? They were above the clouds, which glided swiftly across the northern face of the mountain, as Odell told us – above those clouds that hid his view of them from below. Their atmosphere was a clear one. Cannot you imagine, knowing the spirit of both, that with the view of half the world below them they were so thrilled that they just HAD to go on?

During the weeks and months that followed the expedition's return to England, Odell's description of his last sighting of Mallory and Irvine was subjected to the most minute scrutiny. There was a particular argument over precisely where on the north-east ridge he had last seen the two climbers. In his dispatch to *The Times*, written a few days after the event while the vision was still clear in his mind, Odell said that he saw the two climbers emerging at the top of the second, higher and more difficult of two rock steps which barred progress along the ridge. Doubts have been expressed ever since over whether Mallory and Irvine could have climbed an obstacle as severe as the Second Step appeared to be. But subsequent expeditions, which in recent years have successfully climbed the north-east ridge to the summit, have found that the First Step may be bypassed in its entirety, and that half the height of the Second Step is avoided when it is approached directly from the ridge itself.

The Chinese expedition of 1960 climbed the difficult upper portion of the Second Step by one climber standing on the shoulders of his companion; but it took them many attempts and three hours to achieve success. The 1975 Chinese expedition used an aluminium ladder, which they left in place for the use of all subsequent climbers. In 1985 a Catalan expedition successfully followed the north-east ridge although, in conditions of deep snow, it took them fourteen hours to reach the summit from their Camp VI near the north-east shoulder, and on their return they had to bivouac at the foot of the Second Step. It was their opinion that it was quite possible for Mallory and Irvine to have reached the summit, but that they would not have had sufficient time to return to their camp.

Interest in the fate of Mallory and Irvine, and speculation over their possible success, has continued unabated for eighty years. Prior to 1999 there was just one piece of firm evidence. Members of the 1933 Everest expedition came upon an ice-axe lying on the slabs about 60 feet below the crest of the north-east ridge. Its bright steel head clearly bore the maker's name – Willisch of Tasch. No one but Mallory and Irvine had ever been here before – it must have belonged to one of them. The axe was shown to Odell who was struck by its undamaged condition, showing that it could not have fallen far, if at all. He also noted a triple nick cut into the shaft. It has since been established that this was a mark of identification used by Andrew Irvine. Similar marks were found on his school OTC swagger-stick, which came to light at the time of his father's death in 1962. Writing in the *Alpine Journal*, Odell commented on the implications of the find:

> The actual position where the axe was found was on a gently inclined slab about 200 yards east of the First Step and about 60 feet below the crest of the NE arête. [...] I consider it unlikely that the position of the axe marks the scene of an accident, at any rate on the ascent. It was above this place that I feel sure I saw Mallory and Irvine. Where the axe was found the rocks are very easy, of gentle inclination. It seems to me very possible that one of them – and more plausibly Irvine, less used to carrying an axe on a rock-climb than Mallory – may have decided to leave his axe on the ridge during the ascent, to be picked up on the descent, in view of the climbing being almost entirely on rock under the prevailing conditions.
>
> Alternatively [...] the axe, if retained for the ascent, might [...] have been dropped accidentally, at the spot where found, in the course of their descent in the dark, when it is likely that they would have been roped together.
>
> One speculation is perhaps as good an another, but all things considered I find myself quite unable to conclude that the place where the axe was retrieved was the scene of an accident during Mallory and Irvine's ascent. If its position marks a disaster on their descent, the case would more nearly fit in with my observations on June 8 1924, and would still allow of the possibility that they may have reached the summit.

In the autumn of 1979 a curious twist was given to the story. Wang Hongbao, a Chinese climber who was assisting a Japanese recon-naissance expedition on the North Face, was climbing up to the expedition's Camp III in company with Ryoten Hasegawa, one of the Japanese climbers. When Hasegawa asked him whether he had seen the body of Maurice Wilson, an eccentric Englishman who had died in a solo attempt on Everest in 1934 and whose body had been discovered on several occasions near Camp III, Wang replied that he had done so (when he was a member of a Chinese reconnaissance expedition in 1965). But he then pointed up to the north-east ridge and said: 'Eight thousand, one hundred metre... Engleese.' Wang did not speak Japanese but the two managed to converse through gestures and by writing in the snow.

It emerged that four years earlier, on the 1975 Chinese expedition to the mountain, Wang had gone for a short walk from the expedition's Camp IV at 26,575ft (8100m) and had found the body of a foreign climber. Through hand signals he indicated that the body was lying as if asleep, wearing old fashioned and tattered clothing which disintegrated when touched. Wang pecked his cheek with his finger, from which Hasegawa understood that the cheek was sunken or pecked by birds, and he also indicated that its mouth was open. To make sure that he had not misunderstood Wang, Hasegawa wrote in the snow '8100m – dead English body' and Wang nodded vigorously. Hasegawa knew that only two climbers had died above 8100m before 1975: Mallory and Irvine. Hasegawa intended to ask Wang for further details, but sadly he never got the chance. On the very next day he was ascending to the North Col with Wang and two other Chinese climbers when they were caught in an avalanche. Hasegawa managed to arrest his fall and escaped with five broken ribs, but the three Chinese climbers were killed.

The year 1999 marked the seventy-fifth anniversary of the disappearance of Mallory and Irvine, and in April that year a highly organised attempt was made to find a definitive answer to this intriguing mystery. The Mallory and Irvine Research Expedition, composed mainly of American climbers together with a camera team from the BBC, arrived at base camp with the specific aim of finding the body described by Wang Hongbao. The leader of the expedition was the experienced Himalayan climber and guide Eric Simonson, and their strategy was based on the meticulous planning of Jochen Hemmleb, a twenty-eight-year-old geology student from Frankfurt. For years Hemmleb had been obsessed by the mystery of Mallory and Irvine, and he had come to the conclusion that, if the site of the 1975 Chinese Camp VI could be discovered, a controlled search might be made for the body discovered by Wang Hongbao. After an exhaustive study of previous expedition photographs, compared with detailed maps of the North face of Everest, Hemmleb deduced that the Chinese Camp VI was sited on a rib of rock some distance away from the modern route to the summit. The presumed site of the body mentioned by Wang was to the south-west of the Chinese Camp VI and below the crest of the north-east ridge where the ice-axe (assumed to be Irvine's) had been

found in 1933. It had always been assumed in the mountaineering
world that the body, if discovered would be that of Andrew Irvine.

On 1 May 1999 a search team of six climbers began scouring the
North Face, working at different levels to ensure maximum coverage.
At 11.45 a.m., the American climber, Conrad Anker, who had taken
a lower route than the others, saw 'a patch of white that was whiter
than the rock around it and whiter than the snow'. As he got nearer
he realised that this was a body, and the presence of a hobnailed boot
was proof that it dated back to the 1924 expedition. *Ghosts of Everest,*
the 1999 expedition book, describes what he found as follows:

> This body was lying fully extended, face down and pointing uphill, frozen
> in a position of self-arrest, as if the fall had happened only moments earlier.
> The head and upper torso were frozen into the rubble that had gathered
> around them over the decades, but the arms, powerfully muscular still,
> extended above the head to strong hands that gripped the mountainside,
> flexed fingertips dug deep into the frozen gravel. The legs were extended
> downhill. One was broken and the other had been gently crossed over it for
> protection. The entire body had about it the strength and grace of a dancer.
> This body, this man, had once been a splendid specimen of humankind.

As the climbers gathered round the body they assumed that they had
found the remains of Andrew Irvine. It was only when they turned
over a shirt collar and saw the name tag G. Leigh Mallory that they
realised the truth. In Dave Hahn's words:

> Then it finally hit us: we had not found Andrew Irvine. We had not discov-
> ered Wang Hongbao's 'English dead'. We were in the presence of George
> Mallory himself.

After discussing whether it was right for them to disturb the body,
the climbers came to the conclusion that, if they could find evidence
that Mallory and Irvine had made it to the summit, George Mallory
would want the world to know. The families of Mallory and Irvine
had earlier given their support for the search and for photographing
what was found. Proceeding very carefully, they chipped away with

their ice axes to free the jacket and gain assess to its contents. They worked almost in silence. As Andy Politz commented:

> There was a deep feeling of reverence. We were walking a very fine line, trying to do a responsible job archaeologically while still treating the body itself with the dignity it deserved. This was one of our great heroes, after all, and in an odd sense we felt were working with Mallory the person, not Mallory the body. It was humbling.

After they had recovered all the artefacts, they scoured the steep slope for three quarters of an hour, searching for rocks they could pry up on order to cover the body in burial. Before they left the scene one of the climbers read Psalm 103 and a Church of England committal service, provided by the Bishop of Bristol. As Jake Norton said later:

> It seems an odd thing to say, but I don't think any of us wanted to leave him. We were very comfortable being with 'George'. We wanted to spend more time with him; he was so impressive to be with even in death.

The items they brought down with them included several perfectly preserved letters with their envelopes and a bill from Gamages of London; a pair of nail scissors in a leather case; a tin of 'Brand's and Co.'s Savory Meat Lozenges'; a burgundy handkerchief with the monogram GLM; a fingerless glove; a pocket knife; a box of matches, still usable; an altimeter; a pair of sun goggles (in his pocket); and scraps of paper with pencilled lists of gear. A second search sixteen days later also uncovered Mallory's wristwatch (found in one of his pockets) with the minute hand missing. The letters were from his brother Trafford, his sister Mary and also a friend named Stella. Subsequent investigation has shown that she was Stella Cobden-Sanderson. George had known her former husband, Ferdinand Speyer, who had been a member of Geoffrey Young's climbing parties at Pen y Pass. At one time she had been a buyer for the Peter Jones department stores and she had met George on his American lecture tour when she was on a visit to the USA. He had used the envelope of her letter to make what Hemmleb and the team archaeologist Rick Reanier later realised was a check list of the available oxygen cylinders. The lists of gear showed the detailed preparations he had made for the climb, including reference to six spare oxygen cylinders, which suggests that they had much more oxygen capacity than has been generally realised.

Another important find made by the expedition was the discovery of a 1924 oxygen bottle wedged beneath a big boulder at 27,800ft, about 600ft below the First Step. Eric Simonson had first stumbled on this bottle during a 1991 expedition to the mountain, but unaware of its full significance he had left it where it was. After being recovered by Tap Richards, Hemmleb immediately recognised it as one of the 1924 bottles. The position where it was found proved that Mallory and Irvine had chosen the crest of the ridge for their line of ascent, at least as far as the base of the First Step.

Jochen Hemmleb also made one other significant observation, as he was following the progress of the expedition's summit party from Base Camp through a 600mm camera lens. After gaining the top of the Second Step, the two climbers, Conrad Anker and Dave Hahn, made their way to the foot of another barrier, a broken bastion of rock at 28,550 feet that is now referred to as the Third Step. Hahn later wrote of this barrier:

> It has none of that airy, exposed feeling that the others do; it's more a scramble than a technical climb.

It only took Ankers and Hahn fifteen minutes to climb the Third Step. Watching from below Hemmleb was amazed to realise that what he was looking at was an exact replay of Odell's description of his last sighting of Mallory and Irvine:

> One tiny black spot silhouetted on a small snow-crest beneath a rock-step in the ridge; the black spot moved. Another black spot became apparent and moved up the snow to join the other on the crest. The first then approached the great rock-step and shortly emerged at the top; the second did likewise.

Hemmleb later commented:

I was watching from almost exactly the same angle Odell had, though farther below. It was only after I'd swapped a doubling lens and could see the colour of their down suits that I could be sure I hadn't simply stepped back in time seventy-five years! Now it seemed possible, perhaps even likely, that Odell had seen Mallory and Irvine at the Third Step, not the Second.

Odell was never certain at which of the steps he last saw Mallory and Irvine. A majority of modern climbers believes that the pair could not have surmounted the Second Step in 1924, making a sighting at the higher Third Step implausible. Yet the parallels between Odell's account and the topography of the Third Step are nonetheless striking.

Two years later, in March 2001 the Mallory and Irvine Research Expedition returned to the mountain in an attempt to find the body of Andrew Irvine. The expedition was again led by Eric Simonson and supported by the research of Jochen Hemmleb. Although they did not find Irvine's body they made several significant discoveries. Among the objects found were four oxygen bottles from the 1922 expedition. On the site of the 1922 Camp III they found various remains including rusted tins, parts of wooden packing cases, a few solid-fuel burners and several old zinc-carbon batteries. The expedition also found the remains of Camp VI of the British 1933 expedition. Inside the tent there were various items of food including Nestlé's condensed milk, Heinz spaghetti, Kendal Mint Cake and, with an endorsement from Ernest Shackleton, a partially eaten box of Huntley and Palmer's Superior Reading biscuits. Amazingly, these biscuits were still edible after sixty-eight years! Among the items of equipment were cooking pots, Meta stoves, a cup, a tin opener, a tablespoon with chunks of chocolate still adhering to it, and a candle.

They also identified the site of the 1924 Camp VI, from which Norton and Somervell had made their historic climb to 28,000 feet without oxygen, and Mallory and Irvine had set out on their last attempt. Here, in addition to the remains of the tent, their finds included a yellow-green wool mitten, similar to Mallory's glove found in 1999, an olive-coloured cotton sock bearing Edward Norton's name, two leather straps, some matches, a few chunks of solid fuel, a diffuser from an electric torch and a tin labelled 'Acid Drops', which was found to contain some fragrant tea leaves. They also found a piece of rubber tubing, possibly from an oxygen set. The site of the camp lay only 300 yards from the spot where Mallory's body had been found, showing that he had been close to safety at the time when he fell.

They also discovered the remains of Camp VI of the Chinese 1960 expedition at 26,640ft (8120m) and also that of their 1975 expedition at 26,800ft (8170m). The latter was the very camp from which Wang Hongbao had found his 'Engleese dead'. The site was identified by two oxygen bottles typical for the 1975 expedition and a survey tripod marked 1975. After this important discovery they scoured the area in an attempt to retrace Wang's short walk from the camp, but they found nothing. The 1975 camp was sited 65ft above and 150 yards to the east of the spot where Mallory's body had been buried. This raises the possibility that it was Mallory's body which Wang had found, although, since the body was found face-down in the gravel, Wang could not have seen his face.

There is one further twist to this epic story. After completion of the 2001 expedition, Jochen Hemmleb accompanied Eric Simonson on a visit to Beijing, where they were able to interview some of the veteran members of the Chinese 1960 expedition which, apart from the unknown achievement of Mallory and Irvine, was the first to climb Mount Everest from the north. The Chinese claim to have reached the summit in 1960 was at first regarded with extreme scepticism in the Western World, mainly due to the improbably heroic nature of their climb and also to the lack of photographic evidence. But in the intervening years, as further details have become known, their account has been generally accepted. In addition to finding the site of their Camp VI, the 2001 expedition also discovered their high camp, Camp VII at 27,750ft.

The account of the successful 1960 Chinese expedition reveals a struggle with the mountain of truly epic proportions. On 24 May 1960 four climbers, Xu Jing, Wang Fuzhou, Liu Lienman and a Tibetan named Gonbu, set out from their high camp at 7 a.m. in an attempt on the summit. Soon after leaving camp Xu Jing began to show symptoms of altitude sickness and his place was taken by the expedition's high-altitude cameraman, Qu Yinhua. They reached the Second Step at noon and then wrestled with the 15ft crux for three hours before finally managing to reach the top of the cliff by a combination of the use of pitons and of a human ladder, whereby Qu Yinha after taking off his crampons and boots stepped on the shoulders of Liu Lienman. After gaining another 300ft it became clear that Liu could continue no further. The other three helped him to a shelter in the rock and, after much deliberation, and on Liu's orders, they decided to continue to the summit.

Overcome by darkness they struggled on and finally reached their goal at 2.20 a.m. on 25 May. After remaining fifteen minutes on the summit they started on their descent and at 7.30 a.m. they rejoined Liu Lienman. He had miraculously survived the night, partly by using oxygen. Qu Yinhua now managed to work his movie camera sufficiently to take some pictures, including shots of the final pyramid. After a short rest in deteriorating weather, they struggled back to the top of the Second Step, abseiled down the cliff and reached their high camp at 7 p.m. Even now their ordeal was not over. On the next day, although Gonbu and Liu Lienman managed to get down to the North Col in safety, Qu Yinhua and Wang Fuzhou lagged behind and got separated from them. Near Camp VI Qu slipped and dragged Wang down with him. Both would have fallen to their deaths if the rope had not snagged on a protruding rock. They managed to reach the deserted Camp VI and, after a miserable night, they were escorted down to the North Col by a rescue party the next day.

In Beijing in 2001, Hemmleb and Simonson were able to meet some of the members of the 1960 expedition, among them Wang Fuzhou and Qu Yinhua, who had both reached the summit, and the deputy leader Xu Jing. Wang and Qu described the events of the climb, and showed great emotion when telling of their struggles to overcome the Second Step and of their nearness to death when falling on the descent. Hemmleb and Simonson asked them whether they had found any traces of the Mallory and Irvine climb in 1924. They said that they had found a tent which, from its altitude and position, would seem to have been the 1924 Camp VI. And then showing emotion of the utmost intensity, Xu Jing burst out with what proved to be an astounding declaration. The translator reported his words:

At that time he looked [...] there is a body 8,200 metres high, one body in
a sleeping bag. That person is frozen there.

On further questioning Xu said that he now thought that the altitude was 8,300m (27,230ft) and he persisted in saying that the body
was lying on his back in a sleeping bag, most of which had rotted
away. He estimated the body was about 300m (330 yards) away from
the Chinese Camp VII. Hemmleb and Simonson reflected on this
astounding assertion. They subsequently learned that Xu Jing had been
on his own when he made the find during a climb from the Chinese
Camp VI to Camp VII, because he had lagged behind his group. This
might account for the fact that no other climbers had seen the body.
Xu might also have mistaken layers of tattered and disintegrating
clothing for the remains of a sleeping bag, which it is unlikely that
Mallory and Irvine would have taken on their summit attempt.

On the next day Hemmleb and Simonson were able to meet Wu
Peilan, the widow of Wang Hongbao, the climber who had said that
he had found the body of an 'Engleese dead' on the Chinese expedition of 1975. She was shown a copy of *Ghosts of Everest*, the 1999
expedition book, and after finding the pictures of Mallory's body
immediately said:

You know, my husband told me he had found the old body of a foreign
mountaineer beside a stone back in 1975.

Later that day Hemmleb and Simonson were also able to meet
Zhang Junyan, who had shared a tent at Camp VI with Wang Hongbao
in 1975. He could not remember any further details of where Wang
had gone for his short walk from the camp, but he did remember how
Wang had told him later, at Base Camp, how he had found the body
of a foreigner two days earlier during his walk.

It seems clear from the evidence given by Wang Hongbao and Xu
Jing that members of Chinese expeditions had *twice* found a body
high up on the North Face of Everest. Wang Hongbao said that the
'Engleese body' which he discovered in 1975 was at 26,575ft (8,100m).
The body of a foreign mountaineer which Xu Jing came across in

1960 was clearly at a greater height, at around 27,230ft (8,300m). It would seem that, if these accounts are accepted, the body found by Wang Hongbao in 1975 was, despite some discrepancies in his evidence, that of George Mallory, found again in 1999 at 26,760ft (8,155m). If this is so, the body discovered by Xu Jing could only be that of Andrew Irvine.

The dramatic discovery of Mallory's body in 1999, and the possible sighting of Irvine's last resting place in 1960, fascinating and poignant though they are, do not provide the answer as to whether or not Mallory and Irvine reached the summit. The 2001 expedition did not find the camera which Mallory had been carrying, a collapsible Kodak Vestpocket camera, lent him for the summit attempt by Howard Somervell. Only the discovery of this camera and the development of a summit shot would provide conclusive proof. But the circumstances in which the body was found provide an indication of the nature of the tragedy. It seems to have happened on the way down, perhaps late in the day. Mallory's sun goggles were in his pocket and he appears to have been roped to his partner at the time of his fall. The nature of his injuries seems to indicate that he had not fallen far, probably from well down the face of the Yellow Band below the north-east ridge and tantalisingly close to the safety of Camp VI. When the rope between them broke, Irvine, probably also injured, was left alone on the mountain. He may well have struggled a little way in the direction of Camp VI before sitting down and slipping away from life.

In the absence of any further evidence it must remain a matter for conjecture whether George Mallory and Andrew Irvine succeeded in reaching the summit on 8 June 1924. The 1999 expedition members were divided about this but felt it remained a possibility. After the 2001 expedition Jochen Hemmleb and Eric Simonson concluded:

> Perhaps one day the mountain will reveal additional pieces of the puzzle to complete the picture of Mallory and Irvine's final day. Until then, nobody will know for certain what happened on June 8, 1924.

'One speculation is perhaps as good as another.' Exasperating though it may seem, Noel Odell's words are still true today. The fate of

George Mallory and Andrew Irvine, and the question of whether they succeeded in reaching the summit, must remain veiled in mystery. Perhaps the last word is best left to George Mallory's daughter, Clare, writing in her introduction to the 1999 Expedition book, *Ghosts of Everest*:

> The climbers also found letters from family and friends in his pocket. What they did not find, however, was a picture of my mother. I have a childhood memory of being told that he carried such a picture to place on the summit. Did the fact that it was missing mean he had, indeed, experienced the joy of knowing he had reached the world's highest point before he died? The mystery remains – perhaps it is more interesting that way!

★   ★   ★

On 14 May 1995 George Mallory (George's grandson) reached the summit of Everest by the Mallory route. Reflecting on his achievement he later wrote:

> A moment infused with the deepest meaning swept over me. I placed a photograph of my grandparents in the summit snow, knowing my grandfather would have been proud of me.

BIBLIOGRAPHY

Breashears, David, and Salkeld, Audrey. *Last Climb: The Legendary Everest Expeditions of George Mallory*. National Geographic, Washington 1999

Bruce, C.G., et al. *The Assault of Mount Everest: 1922*. Edward Arnold, 1923

Carr, Herbert (ed.). *The Irvine Diaries*. Gaston-West Col Publications, 1979

Firstbrook, Peter. *Lost on Everest: The Search for Mallory and Irvine*. BBC, 1999

Gillman, Peter and Leni. *The Wildest Dream*. Headline, 2000

Graves, Robert. *Goodbye to all that*. Jonathan Cape, 1929

Green, Dudley. *Mallory of Everest*. Faust, 1991

Greene, Raymond. *Moments of Being*. Heinemann, 1974

Hemmleb, Jochen, Johnson, Larry A. and Simonson, Eric R. *Ghosts of Everest*. Macmillan, 1999

Hemmleb, Jochen, and Simonson, Eric R. *Detectives on Everest*. The Mountaineers Books, 2002

Holzel, Tom, and Salkeld, Audrey. *The Mystery of Mallory and Irvine*. Pimlico, 1999

Howard-Bury, C.K., et al. *Mount Everest: The Reconnaissance 1921*. Edward Arnold, 1921

Keay, John. *The Great Arc*. HarperCollins, 2000

Lubbock, Percy (ed.). *The Diary of Arthur Christopher Benson*. Hutchinson, 1926

Mallory, George. *Boswell the Biographer*. Smith, Elder & Co., 1912

Murray, William. *The Story of Everest*. Dent, 1953

Norton, E.F., et al. *The Fight for Everest: 1924*. Edward Arnold, 1925

Noel, J.B.L. *Through Tibet to Everest*. Edward Arnold, 1927

Noel, Sandra. *Everest Pioneer: the Photographs of Captain John Noel*. Sutton Publishing, 2003

Pye, David. *George Leigh Mallory, a Memoir*. Oxford University Press, 1927

Robertson, David. *George Mallory*. Faber, 1969

Ruttledge, Hugh. *Everest 1933*. Hodder & Stoughton, 1934

Somervell, T. Howard. *After Everest*. Hodder & Stoughton, 1936

Styles, Showell. *Mallory of Everest*, Macmillan, New York, 1967

Summers, Julia. *Fearless on Everest: The Quest for Sandy Irvine*, Weidenfeld & Nicolson, 2000

Tyndale, H.E.G. *Mountain Paths*. Eyre & Spottiswoode, 1948

Young, Geoffrey Winthrop. *On High Hills: Memories of the Alps*. Methuen, 1927

—. *Mountains with a Difference*. Eyre & Spottiswoode, 1951

Younghusband, Sir Francis. *The Epic of Mount Everest*, Edward Arnold, 1926

INDEX